THE HEART
OF SOCIAL
PSYCHOLOGY

THE HEART
OF SOCIAL
PSYCHOLOGY

by

ARTHUR ARON
University of Santa Clara

ELAINE N. ARON
Chapman College

Lexington Books

D.C. Heath and Company · Lexington, Massachusetts · Toronto

Library of Congress Cataloging-in-Publication Data

Aron, Arthur.
The heart of social psychology.

Bibliography: p.
Includes index.
1. Social psychology. I. Aron, Elaine. II. Title.
HM251.A788 1986   302   85–40317
ISBN 0–669–10989–4 (alk. paper)

Published simultaneously in Canada
Printed in the United States of America
International Standard Book Number: 0–669–10989–4
Library of Congress Catalog Card Number: 85–40317

The paper used in this publication meets
the minimum requirements of American National Standard
for Information Sciences—Permanence of Paper
for Printed Library Materials, ANSI Z39.48–1984.

The last numbers on the right below
indicate the number and date of printing.

10 9 8 7 6 5 4 3 2 1

95 94 93 92 91 90 89 88 87 86

Contents

Introduction

Social psychology is a big, busy discipline. But deep at its center there is a heart. This heart only appears between the lines in social psychology journals and textbooks. But it is there, in its traditions, in its researchers, in their relationships. The purpose of this book is to reveal that heart, to let you see what the field feels like to those who have devoted their lives to it. Along the way, we would like to give you some informal descriptions of social psychology's major findings. These are also part of its heart.

This book began as a personal account, based on our impressions over the last seventeen years. But we saw right away that we needed to buttress our impressions with the experiences of others, so we looked for more data. That is, like most work in social psychology, the project developed into something bigger, more inclusive, and more social.

First we read: Kurt Lewin's biography, Fritz Heider's autobiography, and the delightful contributions by social psychologists to Edwin Boring and Gardner Lindzey's *A History of Psychology in Autobiography*. Next we read Richard Evans's interviews in *The Making of Social Psychology* and David Cohen's in *Psychologists on Psychology*, as well as various histories of the field, such as Gordon Allport's classic in the *Handbook of Social Psychology*, Ivan Steiner's chapter in *The First Century of Experimental Psychology*, several articles by Dorwin Cartwright, and Leon Festinger's volume of *Retrospectives on Social Psychology*. Then there was the "crisis" literature from the seventies, when social psychologists wrote long, impassioned articles to each other about where social psychology should be going. And there were also introductions to books, parentheses and asides in articles and chapters, and the *American Psychologist* award presentations and obituaries, all of which proved useful too.

It occurred to us, however, that we ought to check our hypotheses about the field with some of our friends who are social psychologists.

So we sat and talked with them, took a few notes, and began to see that we needed to change strategy again. We needed their ideas. After all, as Dorwin Cartwright (1979) pointed out a few years ago, 90 percent of all the people who have ever been social psychologists are alive today. *They* are the field. The books and the histories are important only in showing how these living social psychologists developed as they have.

We started out chatting with them and jotting sketchy notes, but soon we wanted to save everything on a tape recorder. Similarly, at first we asked whatever came to mind, but over the thirty or so interviews a four-page interview protocol evolved. The best questions, as it turned out, were "How did you get into social psychology?", "When teaching social psychology, is there any overarching theme you try to convey, over and above the specific findings, methods, and theories of the field?", "What makes doing social psychology worthwhile for you?", and "Over and above everything else we have discussed, is there anything else you would tell someone about the field who is considering becoming a social psychologist?"

We also asked for anecdotes and incidents our interviewees remembered about eminent figures in the history of the field or about the studies they had been involved in. Finally, of course, we asked about the characteristics emphasized in each of the chapters of the book.

The questioning was often personal and even pushy: for example, "But why is that meaningful to you?" Yet our respondents were uniformly friendly, helpful, and even enthusiastic about the project. In Ellen Berscheid's opinion, social psychologists are unusually "nice people." From our experience we would certainly agree.

Each interview lasted about an hour. When possible, the interviews were in person—though often at odd times and locales. We met Philip Zimbardo after he gave a talk at the Palo Alto Veterans Administration hospital. We wandered around together for a half hour looking for the canteen to have a soft drink. The tape is full of hospital announcements punctuating Phil's wonderful stories. The interview with Lee Ross was conducted outdoors at a fish and chips restaurant. The interview with Elliot Aronson was carried on over a breakfast we purchased with a two-for-one coupon at a Santa Cruz coffee house. But the vast majority of interviews were conducted over the telephone.[1]

The people we chose to interview were not in any sense meant by us to be a truly representative sample of the field. They consisted of social psychologists who usually but not always met one of the following criteria: (a) were close personal friends; (b) lived near us; (c) had conducted a study we were discussing in the book; (d) had been suggested to us by others; (e) were obviously eminent; or (f) were people we had always wanted to meet.

If persons were *not* interviewed whom readers might have expected us to interview, these were probably persons (a) we could not reach on the phone because they were out of town during the period we were interviewing, (b) who had written autobiographies or had been interviewed at length in some published source, (c) we did not think of, or (d) whose names were at the end of our list when it came time to meet the publication deadline.

We found these interviews delightful and inspiring. We are grateful to those we did talk to, for their time and willingness to cooperate. These are Elliot Aronson, John Arrowood, Solomon Asch, Daryl Bem, Jerry Burger, Ellen Berscheid, Marilyn Brewer, Morton Deutsch, Donald Dutton, Russell Fazio, Barney Gilmore, William Graziano, Anthony Greenwald, O.J. Harvey, Elaine Hatfield, Harold Kelley, Herbert Kelman, Lee Ross, Edward Sampson, Theodore Sarbin, Stanley Schachter, Muzafer Sherif, Jerome Singer, Elizabeth Tanke, Dalmas Taylor, Abraham Tesser, John Touhey, and Philip Zimbardo.

As for the results of all this "research," our conclusions are in our chapter topics: most social psychologists evidence chutzpah (chapter 1); an insistence on the reality of social influence (chapter 2); groups (chapter 3); and cognitions (chapter 5); a personal awareness of those realities (chapter 4); a love of playful research (chapter 6) and intricate theory (chapter 7); and a concern for the world (chapter 8). These seem to be the outstanding characteristics of social psychologists, although certainly not every and possibly not any one social psychologist exhibits them all. But each quality is typical of many in this very heterogeneous field. They also "rang a bell" for those we talked to, seeming typical of others they knew. Perhaps what we have described is a sort of paradigm case of a social psychologist, in the sense of descriptive psychology as used these days by Keith Davis.

We did not, however, intend this little book to be a piece of research. At best, it may be a quasi survey (or perhaps only quasi literature). Our hope is simply that these chapters will seem about right to our colleagues, perhaps verbalizing some things they hadn't thought about and helping their students to appreciate the discipline, culture, and joy behind the formal course offerings. Some of the general public, as well, may be curious about this field, which periodically slips into journalistic prominence.

Instructors who are using this book to teach social psychology may want to assign chapters out of the order in which they appear. For this reason, the chapters were written to be independent and can be used in any order to meet the demands of a course. While the chapter topics do not correspond in an obvious way to textbook topics, they in fact fit fairly well with standard textbook chapters, once we give you the code. For example, chapter 7, which tells the story of the controversy between proponents of cognitive dissonance theory and proponents of self-perception theory, would fit well with a text chapter on attitude change. The appendix offers our suggestions for integrating this book with some of the major, current social psychology textbooks.

For social psychology courses being taught without a full-length textbook, this book should work well with either a short social psychology text, a set of other small books, or a reader of original source material. The book should also be useful as an additional reading in more general courses in psychology, and for certain specific courses, such as the history of psychology, or the sociology or psychology of science.

One final note. We were surprised as we wrote how often it was necessary to refer to Kurt Lewin. We had suspected we would type his name often, and others before us have emphasized him in their books. But we were surprised at the vast extent of his influence, particularly on the motivation and character of the field. The influence of other pioneers in the field is also very strong, especially that of Muzafer Sherif, Ted Newcomb, and Fritz Heider. But Lewin permeates almost everything we have to say.

We are now more convinced than ever that Kurt Lewin was the seminal figure for modern social psychology. We are sorry we could not have interviewed him. But through his students and his student's students we have developed a sincere affection for a man who died when we were two years old. Our hope is that the field will continue to develop in the ways that he pioneered, and that it will fulfill his inspiring vision of its potential both as a science and a way to better the world. We also like to think that he would have enjoyed this book. We definitely hope you do.

Note

1. We used state-of-the-art technology and controlled laboratory conditions. We hung the cheapest Radio Shack microphone from a desk lamp so it dangled an inch above our speaker phone. The recordings came out quite well, although the interviewees thought we were asking our questions from a tunnel. Also, our phone has "call waiting," so some interviews were interrupted by urgent calls from our teenage son. Hal Kelley graciously accommodated to three such interruptions in a half hour. Then there was the one interview with one particularly interesting character which simply didn't get onto the tape, for reasons we can only assume were providential.

1
Chutzpah

CHUTZPAH is a Yiddish word meaning the guts to stick your neck out, perhaps even a little *too* far out, and take on something really big. Social psychologists abound in chutzpah, confidently believing that any social question worth debating is worth testing rigorously, if possible with an experiment in a "social psychology laboratory." No area of human concern, from the most pressing practical problems to the most long-standing philosophical issues, is beyond the reach of some determined social psychologist.

A prime example (among thousands) is Stanley Schachter. In the opinion of many he is the outstanding social psychologist at work today. So far in his prolific and audacious career he has studied why people want to be with others, how people know what they feel, what makes people overweight, why people commit crimes, and why people smoke. All these are areas that have stymied other researchers, and the public, for years. One of his most recent projects is figuring out how public awareness of violence through the media affects whether people will go out of their homes—for example, to shop. This new area he calls the study of *psychological aggregates*.

Whatever the project, in each case Schachter quickly makes breakthroughs. He has humbly explained how: "There's no such thing as a tough area. An area's tough only if you don't have an idea" (quoted in Evans, 1976, p. 166). When pressed, Schachter admitted,

> It's hard to talk about some of these things without sounding pompous. But if I were forced to give advice, I'd say, get problem-oriented, follow your nose and go where problems lead you. Then if something opens up that's interesting and that requires techniques and knowledge with which you're unfamiliar, learn them. (p. 168)

It's that simple when you have chutzpah.

Kurt Lewin—Chutzpah versus Hitler

Schachter was first a student of Kurt Lewin, then of one of Lewin's prize students, Leon Festinger. Through Schachter, Festinger, and numerous others, Kurt Lewin was the single greatest influence on social psychology. Nearly every major trend in social psychology—group dynamics, cognitive dissonance, attribution theory—has been primarily developed by a student or close associate of Kurt Lewin. After Lewin's death in 1947, the great learning psychologist Edward Tolman wrote:

> Freud, the clinician, and Lewin, the experimentalist, these are the two men who will always be remembered because of the fact that their contrasting but complementary insights first made of psychology a science which was applicable both to real individuals and to real society. (1948, p. 26)

Yet Lewin has hardly achieved the psychic demigod status of Freud. Lewin's theory is no longer widely used in social psychology, and his name appears on only a few research studies. So what was his great influence?

Lewin role-modeled chutzpah (and most of the other qualities of social psychology discussed in this book).

Lewin came to America—to Iowa, the heartland—in the mid-1930s. He was fleeing Hitler, and while Lewin was a gentle person, he could also be stubborn. Loving democracy deeply, he set out to attack tyranny the best way he knew, through the new science of social psychology.

Lewin's commitment to democracy was more than abstract political ideology. His very style of *doing* science was democratic, and very effective. As we said, Lewin's influence was not mainly from his own personal theories or research. It wasn't even from his lectures. It was from his *Quasselstrippe* (a German word roughly meaning "bull session"), where he sat around chatting with his students and playing with ideas. As their organizer and informal leader, he showed consistent respect and warmth. Whether he was listening to an undergraduate or an eminent colleague, everyone's ideas received a hearing. Lewin was enormously brilliant and creative, but what stood out was his ability to facilitate brilliance and creativity in those around him, especially through his enthusiastic and democratic intellectual leadership.[1]

While Lewin was noted for his good humor, on one subject he was vehement. That, of course, was democracy. Robert Sears, a well-known developmental theorist and colleague of Lewin's at the University of Iowa, commented about Lewin, "The autocratic way he insisted on democracy was a little spectacular. . . . There was nothing to criticize—but one could not help noticing the fire and the emphasis" (quoted in Marrow, 1969, p. 127).

With such fire, it was not surprising that when one of Lewin's new graduate students, Ronald Lippitt, asked about studying the effect of different kinds of leadership structures, Lewin immediately abandoned his other research plans and plunged into the idea enthusiastically. Together with Lippitt, and later Ralph White as well, Lewin constructed an ingenious series of experiments to compare scientifically the effects of autocratic versus democratic leadership.

It was a revolutionary idea to take this age-old question of practical affairs and social philosophy and subject it to rigorous scientific scrutiny. Lewin was adamant, however, that all of life was the domain of the new science of social psychology. Nothing need be left to speculation and argument. Experimental research would solve the perennial problems of humankind.

The experiment itself was elegantly simple. The subjects were eleven-year-old boys who had volunteered to participate. The researchers organized them into several "clubs" of five boys each, each group a similar composite of personalities (based on teachers' assessments). The clubs chose names such as "Sherlock Holmes," "Dick Tracy," "Secret Agents," and "Charlie Chan." Each club was assigned an adult leader to help it carry out its crafts, games, and so forth over the next twenty weeks of meetings. To assess what went on in the groups, during each meeting several researchers observed. The boys and their parents were also interviewed later about the groups. The groups differed in only one respect—the behavior of the adult leaders.

Initially the leaders adopted one of two styles. One was *autocratic*, in which the leader took charge of every aspect of the tasks, kept the boys in the dark about the next step, and generally maintained complete authority at all times. The other was *democratic*, in which the leader encouraged group discussion and decision making and saw that during each step of an activity the boys were aware of that step's purpose in achieving the activity's overall goal.

Later, when Ralph White came to Iowa as a postdoctoral fellow in political science, he could not resist joining the social psychologists' research team. When White attempted to play the democratic leader, however, Lippitt and Lewin noted that his version of the democratic leader was quite different from the others'. Rather than changing White's approach to the role, Lewin realized White was really demonstrating a third important leader type: *laissez faire*, in which the leader plays a completely passive role, allowing members to do as they please and interfering as little as possible.

Thus, in its final form the study compared three leadership styles and the social climates surrounding them. Great care was taken to make the leaders' behaviors similar in all other ways—for example, how much joking and kindness they expressed. Each club experienced more than one kind of leader, in a systematic rotation.

The result was clear. Under autocratic leadership the groups' behaviors fell into one of two general styles: passive and dependent or hostile and resistant. Either way, the autocratic groups' members were less satisfied and less friendly with one another in and out of the group.

With democratic leadership there was the greatest independence, least discontent, and most friendliness in and out of the group. Moreover, during activities members cooperated more and concentrated more on getting their task done.

The laissez-faire group was closer to the democratic than the autocratic groups in many ways, except they were considerably more apathetic and less work-oriented.

Perhaps the most interesting differences emerged during "test episodes." In one, the experimenters arranged for the leader to come late. On their own, the democratic groups worked well; the authoritarian groups simply stopped doing much of anything; and the laissez-faire groups were active, but not very effective in their activities.

In another test episode the experimenters sent in a stranger (a "janitor" or "electrician") while the leader was out, to criticize the group and its members. The authoritarian groups responded with much more hostility, perhaps showing a "scapegoating" effect.

Almost all the boys preferred the periods in which they had a democratic leader, but the transitions were difficult for most, especially from autocratic to democratic or laissez faire.

Lewin was not shy about drawing conclusions:

On the whole, I think that there is ample proof that the difference in behavior in autocratic and democratic situations is not a result of differences in the individuals. There have been few experiences for me as impressive as seeing the expression on children's faces during the first day under an autocratic leader. The group that had formerly been friendly, open, cooperative, and full of life, became within a short half-hour a rather apathetic-looking gathering without initiative. The change from autocracy to democracy seemed to take somewhat more time than that from democracy to autocracy. Autocracy is imposed on the individual. Democracy he has to learn! (1939, p. 31)

Muzafer Sherif Tackles the Problem of War and Peace

Of course, Lewin was not the only source of chutzpah for social psychology. Another pioneer was Muzafer Sherif, who studied under Gardner Murphy at Columbia University. Murphy was a contemporary of Lewin's; in 1935 he wrote the first modern social psychology text. Later Murphy said social psychology started out as a "relatively well-behaved junior sib among the big boys and girls [of mainstream psychology] who had been around longer and knew better how to accommodate to the academic giants" (1965, p. 24). But, "Some of the creative people refused to work within the psychology that was standard for their era. Think of the rebels like Lewin, Sherif, and Moreno" (p. 24).

And think of Murphy himself, who was just as confident as Lewin that no human folly would dare to persist once psychology had identified what needed to be done. So Murphy passed all this social psychology chutzpah on to his students,[2] including Muzafer Sherif, a young graduate student from Turkey who had come to America to study psychology. (You'll learn all about Sherif's dramatic decision to study social psychology in chapter 8.)

Sherif challenged the way attitudes were measured, and then conducted one of the first studies experimentally delineating the process of the formation of social norms (Sherif, 1935), which you will read about in chapter 3. But of all his contributions, the chutzpah shows through most in a series of three "summer camp" studies (Sherif, Harvey, White, Hood, & Sherif, 1961), culminating in the study subtitled "The Robber's Cave Experiment." This is the study that Sherif told us was, among all his works, "closest to my heart."

At Robber's Cave, Oklahoma, Sherif and his students, O.J. Harvey, B.J. White, and W.E. Hood, modestly set out to study the formation of culture, the causes of intergroup conflict, and the resolution of intergroup enmity. (The results were then written up by his wife, the independently famous social psychologist, Carolyn Wood Sherif.) That is, in a single study, Sherif and company attacked the issues of what creates a society and what causes war and peace.

During the summer of 1954, a number of upper-middle-class eleven- and twelve-year-old boys[3] were invited to attend "a special summer camp" at Robber's Cave. When they arrived, before they even saw each other, they were randomly divided into two groups and sent to different parts of the large campground. For the first few days each group was not even aware of the other's existence. Nevertheless, by the second week, loyalties were strong. Each group had named itself, and both the Eagles and the Rattlers had developed leaders and informal social rules.

As soon as the two groups did hear about each other, each began to challenge the other to competitions. The researchers added fuel to this inherent competitive spark by bringing the two groups together to play team games, including very hard fought tugs-of-war. In all these competitions the winning group received a prize and the loser nothing.

The researchers used every opportunity to increase the losers' frustration. One technique, developed at a similar camp a previous summer, was to give a party after a competition to "let bygones be bygones." The experimenters deliberately arranged for half the refreshments to be "delectable and whole" while the other half were "crushed and unappetizing." One group was brought to the party just earlier enough to allow its members to select, naturally, all the delectable appetizers. When the other group arrived, they were faced with the unappealing leftovers and the spectacle of plates full of good stuff on the laps of their enemies. The late group was hardly pacified by this turn of events.

Even without this encouragement, the groups had developed an ingroup-versus-outgroup mentality. Each group called the members of the other group names and considered them inferior. On a questionnaire, the vast majority of both groups rated their own members as "brave," "tough," and "friendly," and rated the other group's as "sneaky," "smart-alecks," and "stinkers."

But now came the next, too-human stage: war. Fights broke out, flags were stolen, raids undertaken, green apples hoarded for "ammunition." The group structures themselves became all too reminiscent of societies at war, with leadership assigned by the group to the toughest kids and with a great focus on attacks and the "enemy." In fact, the researchers had to intervene several times to avoid bloodshed.

Then began the most challenging part of the study. Having created this microcosm of an intolerant and warring world. Sherif and company set out to create peace. First they tried bringing opposing factions together to share pleasant activities. It didn't work; a joint banquet turned into a food fight.

Another idea was religious services emphasizing peacemaking:

> The topics were brotherly love, forgiveness of enemies, and cooperation. The boys arranged the services and were enthusiastic about the sermon. Upon solemnly departing from the ceremony, they returned within minutes to their concerns to defeat, avoid, or retaliate against the detested out-group. (Sherif & Sherif, 1969, pp. 254–55)

Yet another idea was conferences between the group leaders. But the staff didn't even try to arrange them, given the outcome of a spontaneous attempt of this kind during one of the early experiments:

> A high status [member of one group] went on his own initiative to the [other group's] cabin with the aim of negotiating better relationships. He was greeted by a hail of green apples, chased down the path, and derided. Upon returning to his own group, he received no sympathy. Despite his high status, he was rebuked for making the attempt, which was doomed to failure in the opinion of his fellow members. (p. 255)

So much for summit meetings. In fact, with every attempt to resolve the conflict, whether initiated by the experimenters or the boys themselves, the hostility only seemed to increase. Indeed, in the first two summer-camp studies, the boys went home harboring a good deal of bad feeling against the opposing groups.

Fortunately for everyone, however, during the 1954 camping session at Robber's Cave the experimenters finally found a strategy that worked: they introduced *superordinate goals*. This was done by setting up a series of situations in which the two groups had to cooperate to attain a joint objective. For example, the camp food truck would not start (thanks to the researchers' surreptitious efforts) and all the boys had to pull together, literally, to get the truck going, and on the very rope they had used earlier for vicious tugs-of-war. Another time the water supply "accidentally" broke down and the boys had to work together to locate the problem along a mile of pipe.

Gradually the war ended. By the time camp was over, the two groups actually asked to go home on the same bus. And when the bus stopped for a rest break, the groups decided to pool their prize money so everyone could buy malts.

Sherif and his colleagues were entirely aware of the larger implications of their research. They did not see it as mere "child's play." On the contrary, in their various reports of the experimental results, they emphasized that nations can coexist peacefully only if they develop meaningful joint goals. On the basis of these studies, Sherif has made an impassioned plea:

> The broadening of human bonds is the prerequisite for morality in dealing with peoples outside the narrow in-group bounds, for creation of a widening sense of "we-ness." . . .
>
> The trend is towards larger and larger dependence between peoples and toward the formation of organizations encompassing them. Historical evidence and empirical data of social science support this trend, even though they also show great human wear and tear, suffering, and reverses for intervals of time.
>
> The great question is whether the trend toward interdependence will be permitted to culminate in the standards of conduct required from all, despite stubborn, last-ditch opposition by islands of resistance, or whether the trend will collapse in the world wide holocaust of a thermonuclear showdown. (Sherif, 1966, p. 174)

What other discipline stands ready to conduct research on how to rescue *homo sapiens* from self-extinction? What other discipline would have the chutzpah to draw conclusions about war and peace from research at a summer camp for boys? It may be presumptuous, but it may also be a very good thing that some people are trying. Indeed, most social psychologists would agree that Sherif's study remains our single most important source of scientific knowledge about the causes and cures of group hatred.

Social Psychology Challenges the Boob Tube

In the 1970s, when debate was raging over the impact of violence depicted on television, social psychologists put the issue to an experimental test. This time the chutzpah was international: Jacques-Philippe Leyens at the University of Louvain in Belgium designed the study, along with two associates from the United States and one from Brazil.

Leyens, Camino, Parke, and Berkowitz (1975) disconnected the televisions in four dormitories in a private high school for delinquent or homeless boys (yes, again boys!). This alone should have led to violence. But as a substitute the experimenters provided a special "movie week." Each dormitory saw five films, one each night. In two of the dormitories the boys saw highly violent films, such as *The Dirty Dozen* and *Bonnie and Clyde*. The boys in the other two dormitories saw films without any violence, such as *Lily* and *Daddy's Fiancee*.

During this and the following week, the boys' behavior was observed. Everyone but the major television networks can guess the results: those who saw the violent movies were substantially more violent. While the issue is a complex one, on which a great deal of subsequent research has been done, the findings of this research have been a landmark for understanding this topic.

Social Psychology Challenges the Alleged Apathy of the Whole Human Race

In New York in 1964, Kitty Genovese was brutally murdered while thirty-eight people stood watching. The public was outraged. Why didn't anyone help? How could people be so callous? Amid all the heated discussion, two social psychologists set out to study the question experimentally.

No, they did not stage a murder, although you'll see in the next chapter that some research has come close to doing so. They did simulate the situation enough to provide some solid insights. And in the process, they began a whole new area of research: *prosocial behavior*.

Bibb Latane and John Darley (1970), respectively of Columbia and New York universities, told student volunteers they were participating in an experiment in which they would discuss with one or more other volunteers the problems of living in a big city. This discussion would occur over an intercom because each discussant was (supposedly) in a separate room. Only one person could speak at a time, in a systematic rotation of turns. Finally, the students were told that no one else but the experiment's participants would hear any of the discussion and their identities would remain anonymous.

In actuality, only one student was present for each experimental session. The other "participant" (or in one condition, four others) was actually just a tape recording. This "participant" talked first, describing his problems living in New York—including a special problem of occasional seizures. Next the true subject gave a two-minute talk. Then, in those conditions when others were supposed to be present, the four others talked, again actually on tape.

The subject would then be told there would be a second round of discussion, beginning again with the "participant" who had mentioned the seizures. This time, after the taped voice had spoken normally for a while, he began to stammer, "I er um I think I I need er if if could er er somebody . . . help me out it would . . . er s-s-sure be good . . . uh I've got a a one of the er sei er . . ." and so forth, including choking sounds and ending with "I'm gonna die er . . . help er er seizure er [chokes, then quiet]" (pp. 95–96).

Latane and Darley found that if the students thought they were the only ones listening, 85 percent jumped up and went to the next room to help before the victim had finished. But if they thought there were four other students listening, only 31 percent did so. Thus Latane and Darley discovered a peculiar paradox: the more people who witness a person in need, the less likely it is that any one of them will help.

Social Psychology Sets Out to Resolve the Great Issues of Psychology

Of course, social psychologists do not limit themselves to mundane, practical topics like war and peace. They tackle, with equal aplomb, the Great Issues which have stymied the most brilliant philosophers, essayists, and poets throughout the ages. Love, happiness, life, death—social psychology has hauled them all into some laboratory for experimental analysis.

Love did not become a topic until the late 1960s, not because social psychologists thought it too hard to study, but because many considered it too trivial. A few graduate students felt otherwise. In the early 1960s they had danced to popular songs that vainly asked, "I wonder, wonder, wonder, wonder who/Tell me who wrote the book of love?" In the late 1960s, they wrote the book themselves, after devising some ingenious experiments.

Zick Rubin (who also wrote songs) completed a doctoral dissertation at the University of Michigan in which he found that couples who spent more time gazing into each other's eyes did indeed score higher on a paper-and-pencil questionnaire that Rubin called the "love scale." His 1970 article "The Measurement of Romantic Love" describes this scale.

At about the same time, one of us (A. Aron, 1970), provoked all kinds of havoc as a doctoral student at the University of Toronto by studying love and power. Fortunately his enthusiastic thesis advisor, John Arrowood, was—you guessed it—a former student of Schachter and of other students of Kurt Lewin.

In this study, male student volunteers participated in a series of tasks with an attractive female student they believed to be another experimental subject. Actually, however, she was in league with the experimenter, and the tasks were rigged so that in both physical and verbal conflicts, she either acted strong, weak, or strong and then yielding. As predicted, the subjects were more attracted to the woman in those conditions when she was strong then yielding. (See chapter 6.)

One of the first and most influential studies of love was conducted in the sixties by Elaine Walster and her colleagues (1966) at the University of Wisconsin (she is now Elaine Hatfield and at the University of Hawaii). The goal was to test experimentally whether people are attracted to the best-looking members of the opposite sex or to someone about as attractive as themselves.

While the poets and novelists offered their own answers, and U.S. senators publicly stated that love could not be studied scientifically, Hatfield and her associates invited students to a dance where their dates were to be selected by computer. As the students registered, they were surreptitiously rated for their physical attractiveness by four other students. Then they were "matched" with a date for the dance. Actually, unknown to them, the match was entirely random. During the intermission the students completed questionnaires about how attracted they were to their date. Six months later everyone was contacted again to see if they had tried to go out again with their "match" for the dance.

The findings were unexpected and clear: whether handsome or homely, the students were more likely to try to go out again with the better looking dates.

Subsequent studies have shown that if you have to make your own match, rather than risk rejection, you take care to choose a date about as good-looking as yourself. For example, a few years after this study, Sarah Kiesler and Roberta Baral (1970), as students at Yale, either raised or lowered the self-esteem temporarily of male subjects, by giving them an IQ test and then telling them they had either done very well or very poorly. At that point, the situation was rigged so that the subject had an opportunity to chat alone with a female student who was either very or moderately attractive. As predicted, subjects who had had their self-esteem raised were more likely to ask the female out for a date when they were left with the very attractive student, while those with their self-esteem lowered were more likely to ask out the moderately attractive student.

These studies were just the tip of the iceberg. The study of love exploded into a major subspecialty of social psychology in the seventies and eighties.

If the mysteries of love can be penetrated, why not the vagaries of happiness? Social psychologist Philip Brickman at Northwestern University, along with Dan Coates and Ronnie Janoff-Bulman (1978), took on the eminently philosophical question of whether happiness is relative. In the long run, how does good fortune or tragedy really affect happiness?

They questioned twenty-two people who had recently won major prizes in the Illinois State Lottery, twenty-nine who had recently suffered a serious accident and become paraplegic, and twenty-two ordinary individuals. After an average of six months from the event, the people in all three groups reported themselves to be about equally happy. All averaged above the midpoint on a six-point scale ranging from "not at all" to "very much." And their expectations about their future happiness showed no difference at all.

Social psychology has plunged on through the Forest of Social Evils and the Swamp of Murky Questions. Other psychologists, looking on from behind their rat cages and personality tests, may be hoping this upstart field will eventually "mature." If anything, however, the latest social psychologists are showing more, not less chutzpah. For example, Ellen Langer and Judith Rodin (1976; Rodin & Langer, 1977) decided to study the meaning of life.

Through the centuries, philosophers have speculated that life lasts so long as it has meaning, purpose, free will. Langer and Rodin decided to test this idea experimentally by increasing the meaning in the lives of certain aged residents of a Connecticut nursing home. (If the social psychologists have not matured since Lewin's time, at least the subjects in their experiments have.)

Residents on one floor of the home attended a meeting in which the nursing-home administrator gave a talk emphasizing the control they have over their lives:

> I was surprised to learn that many of you don't . . . realize the influence you have over your own lives here. Take a minute to think of the decisions you can and should be making. For example. . . . This brings me to another point. If you are unsatisfied with anything here, you have the influence to change it. . . . Also, I want to give you each a present. . . . [A box of small plants was passed around, and the patients were given two decisions to make: first, whether or not they wanted a plant at all, and second, to choose which one they wanted. . . .] The plants are yours to keep and take care of as you'd like. . . . One last thing . . . we're showing a movie two nights next week. . . . You should decide which night you'd like to go, if you choose to see it at all. (Langer & Rodin, 1976, pp. 193–194)

Three days later the director visited each patient and repeated parts of the message.

A comparable group of residents on another floor of the same nursing home were treated to a similar meeting and visits, except that for them the message stressed the staff's responsibility for the patients. There was no emphasis on the residents' responsibility, they were given a plant with no choice as to which they would get, they were told the nurses would take care of the plants for them, and they were assigned a movie night.

Three weeks later the residents who had been encouraged to take responsibility for their own lives were happier, more active, and more alert. A year and a half later, these same residents who had received the responsibility message were rated as more vigorous and social by nurses and in better health by doctors. Above all, 85 percent were still alive, whereas only 70 percent were still alive on the other floor.

Kurt Lewin would have loved this study. It is daring. It has social significance. And it shows a lot of chutzpah.

In the next chapter we will focus on one especially significant instance of chutzpah: the daring insistence of social psychologists that we human beings are not rugged, independent individuals, but completely enmeshed in a social field. Every move, every perception, every thought, even about ourselves, is very largely a function of those around us. It has not been a popular stance. But that is no problem when you've got chutzpah.

Notes

1. Everyone we have spoken to who knew Lewin remarked on his enthusiasm. It was so contagious that when he first visited this country in 1929, when he still could speak only German, he developed a following which included some who could not understand a word of his talks. They just liked the man!
2. Murphy continued to be an important figure in psychology, but mainly in the area of personality theory and research.
3. One commentator (MacKinnon, 1949) pointed out that Lewin, and presumably Sherif, worked with children for the same reason that learning psychologists work with rats: they are simpler organisms. (One wonders how many children these researchers knew intimately.) That is, one can see the deeper principles without adult complications. But no doubt another reason was the one which now explains the use of sophomore college students: the kids were available, and they were willing or obliged to do what they were told.

2

"Lemmings Overrule Dissidents and Choose Seashore Conference Site"

I MAGINE you are a skin cell (we know it's ridiculous, but do it). Your job is to toss out bundles of chemicals when told to, to shrivel up tight when told to, to stand your ground when bumped, and generally to keep up your borders. Food and water gets delivered when you need it. Now and then a nice thrill runs through you and your neighbors. When you're in the mood, you reproduce yourself. It's a good life.

But what would you think about the situation? Would you think you were an independent cell, doing your own thing, free to leave when you felt like it, free not to toss out bundles of chemicals if you wanted a day off, free to reproduce yourself ad infinitum? Unless you were very sick, that would not be your self-concept. You would know that you were part of a body. If you left, you would die. If you quit and the others around you quit, the body would die. If you quit and the others did not quit, you would get shoved aside, you would shrivel up, and . . . But you couldn't quit anyway. This is *you*, Skin Cell. Your place is Left Forearm, Human Being. You know no other life.

In a way, social psychology is something of a crusade. Its Holy Grail is to make the people of the world realize that they are part of a social organism, as much as a cell is part of a body, and that they are constantly subject to social influences. To social psychologists, it is as though humans are under some spell which keeps them from seeing this social influence. And as psychologists, they want to break this spell.

Why? Some just want other people to see the truth so that perhaps they will blame individuals less and the situation more when things go wrong. Others hope that people will be able to resist social influence when it would be better to do so, once people can be made to see that influence. Still others hope people will spontaneously do more for the health of the social organism if they see their dependence on it. But whatever the reason, social psychologists strive with a single purpose to make people see, as social psychologist Russ Fazio put it, "the incredible power of the social."

The very definition of the field accepted by most is the study of how people "are influenced by the actual, imagined, or implied presence of others" (G.W. Allport, 1968, p. 3). Social psychologists have demonstrated, through a wide assortment of research which we can only sample here, that this influence determines human thoughts and attitudes, perception, emotions, and even the very self. In fact, some social psychologists say about "self-knowledge" that there is "literally nothing to know" (Gergen, 1977, p. 19), because the "self" or "individual" is simply the sum total of the various social influences to which a person has been exposed.

It takes a lot of chutzpah to embark on such a campaign. In Western cultures especially, people seem to like to think of themselves as rugged individuals who control their own destiny, succeed or fail according to their own efforts, and base their beliefs and feelings, and certainly their perceptions, on direct, rational, "objective" experience. How do you break this spell?

Virtually every social psychologist we interviewed in the process of writing this book described a desire to demonstrate the ubiquity of social influence. The majority said it was their main message to undergraduate students. For example, Ellen Berscheid, an eminent researcher in social perception and 1984 president of the Society for Personality and Social Psychology, said:

> The most important thing I want to get across to students—because they come in with such a bias—is very simply that the kind of person they are depends very much upon the situations in which they find themselves and the social influences that are at work in those situations. They may not be aware of these influences, but they are very real.

Is this a good cause for a crusade? Or something more like tilting at windmills? Do you think you really aren't *quite* as tightly enmeshed in society as a cell is embedded in a body? Then, for a minute, cut yourself free and imagine you are the only person in the world. (Yet you have somehow managed to survive and reach adulthood. Don't ask us how!) Your first thought is probably that you would lack the comforts provided by technology. That is a good point. Science, technology, agricultural techniques—society has developed them all, and passed the knowledge on from generation to generation. But that would be the least of your problems. Your very ability to think about the situation would be extremely limited. How would you think without language? And everything else about living, from eating and drinking to sleeping and waking, would have to be learned from scratch.

Worse, you would probably be listless and lonely, whether you knew why or not (animals raised in total isolation are not very happy looking beasts either). Any meaning to life beyond survival—love, success, power, having your efforts appreciated, even laughter—almost all the pleasures of life are tightly bound up with other people.

You also would know very little. What is poisonous to eat, how long is an inch, where and what your brain is—these are "social realities." That is, you know these things because someone else told you. This authority in turn relied on still others, the few people who actually did the "research." If that much of what we accept to be "objectively" true is really social knowledge, think how much more social are your political and moral "realities," like the importance of democracy or the sacredness of human life.

Got the message? But how would you get it across to others? (Before one of them blows the whole social organism up.) As Ellen Berscheid said, "social influence is one of the great, great influences in nature . . . tremendously powerful . . . yet you can't see it."

Of course, as Berscheid added, you can't see electricity or gravity either. But through ingenious experiments, physicists proved the existence of these basic forces. Similarly, social psychologists have demonstrated the existence of this other basic, powerful, invisible force of nature. The purpose of this chapter is to examine some of the ways they are accomplishing this feat, looking at studies in four areas: how social factors determine how we think, see, feel, and know ourselves. We'll begin with a simple enough study, a pioneering effort by Theodore Newcomb done in 1934 at Bennington College in Vermont, just after the college's founding.

Other People Influence What We Think

The story of how Ted Newcomb became a social psychologist is as clear a case of social influence as his research. Newcomb's father was a minister and Ted Newcomb intended to become a minister too. Except, the seminary he attended was across the street from Columbia University. This was the 1920s and Gardner Murphy was there, talking about this new field of social psychology. (Muzafer Sherif would arrive at Columbia in 1931.) Many of America's other great early psychologists were also at Columbia, for example Edward Thorndike and Robert S. Woodworth.

Also at the seminary, besides Newcomb, were Carl Rogers, Rensis Likert (who later practically invented the opinion survey), and Ernest Hilgard (who was to author a leading text and become an authority on self-theory and hypnosis). Interested in psychology, these seminarians began to spend more and more time at Columbia. The more they associated with one another and with Columbia's psychology graduate students, the less they felt like future theologians and the more they felt like future social scientists. A certain class in "New Testament Exegesis" was the last straw for Newcomb. The professor gave an entire lecture on the meaning of a single Greek word, which he promised to continue explaining during the next class meeting. Newcomb changed schools.

It is not surprising that Ted Newcomb came "to see individual psychological processes within a matrix of group influences" (1974, p. 374).

In 1934 Newcomb took a job teaching at a recently established "experimental" college for women. Bennington College was very exclusive and most of the students were from wealthy, politically conservative families. The faculty, on the other hand, were largely liberal, many even radical. Thanks to the events of the Depression, even Newcomb, the minister's son, voted for Socialist Norman Thomas in the 1932 presidential election. So the women at Bennington were moving from one context—a conservative family and social life—into a new context, where the respected figures, the faculty, held diametrically opposed views.

Newcomb immediately saw his chance to demonstrate in a natural setting his belief that "membership in established groups usually involves the taking on of whole patterns of interrelated . . . attitudes" (1958, p. 265). He spent his first year at Bennington sharpening his lance: his attitude tests. Then in 1935 he launched his version of the social influence crusade by testing the political attitudes of the arriving freshman class. After that, all he had to do was sit back and let the liberal attitudes of the college do its work, and to measure the attitudes of this group of students every year until they graduated.

What he found was very straightforward. With each semester at Bennington, students became increasingly liberal in their politics. By the time they were seniors, and often much sooner, they had totally reversed their political course.

Some were well aware of the process, but it made no difference. For example, one senior explained, "I simply got filled with new ideas here, and the only possible formulation of all of them was to adopt a radical approach" (p. 273). Another said, "I'm easily influenced by people whom I respect, and the people who rescued me when I was down and out, intellectually, gave me a radical intellectual approach" (p. 273). Yet another said, "I was so anxious to be accepted that I accepted the political complexion of the community here" (p. 273).

Those few students who did not change their attitudes were the ones who spent their vacations with their parents, wrote home a lot, and generally maintained their parents' society as their own culture. Newcomb, thanks to some conversations much later with Muzafir Sherif, eventually came to call the group with which one holds common attitudes, one's *reference group*.

Other People Influence What We See

Okay, political attitudes are amorphous. We change them all the time. But how about what we see? Will a 5-inch line look 3 inches long just because our reference group says it is so? According to a study by Solomon Asch, you'd better believe it.

Asch was another Columbia student, sometime after Newcomb and before Sherif. He started out more interested in learning than social psychology. But he was studying with some of the founders of the Gestalt school of psychology, which emphasizes the role of patterns, context, and holistic qualities in perception. Gestalt psychology has always been closely connected to social psychology because of Lewin's insistence that what we see is determined by the *whole* context, including social influences. And when Asch did research on how people perceive each other, it was very *social* research. (We'll discuss this work in chapter 5.) His most famous study, the "Asch conformity study," is what we will describe here, after we tell you about the boyhood experience that led up to it.

Solomon Asch was Jewish, and as a boy had attended more than one Passover seder. If you have ever been to a seder, you know that traditionally a place is set for Elijah the prophet, including a cup of wine. At a certain point in the ceremony the door is opened. Asch recounted to us what happened at this point at one such Seder when he was young:

> I asked my uncle, who was sitting next to me, why the door was being opened. He replied, "The prophet Elijah visits this evening every Jewish home and takes a sip of wine from the cup reserved for him."
>
> I was amazed at this news and repeated, "Does he really come? Does he really take a sip?"
>
> The answer was "Yes." Then my uncle said, "If you watch very closely, when the door is opened you will see—you watch the cup—you will see that the wine will go down a little."
>
> And that's what happened. My eyes were riveted upon the cup of wine. I was determined to see whether there would be a change. And to me it seemed—it was tantalizing, and of course, it was hard to be absolutely sure—that indeed something was happening at the rim of the cup, and the wine did go down a little.

Later, as a researcher, Asch (1958) set up much the same situation with all the proper scientific controls. He seated male students, one at a time, at a table along with seven other male students for what the student thought was a simple experiment in "visual judgment." The task was to determine which of a group of three comparison lines shown on a large card was equal to a standard line shown on a similar card. Each student around the table said, in turn, which of the three comparison lines he thought matched the standard line. Then two more cards were shown, one with three lines, the other with the line to be matched. A total of eighteen cards were shown.

The actual perceptual task was very simple and ordinarily virtually everyone would have instantly agreed on what they saw. Thus, it always came as a considerable surprise to the student subject when on the third card, all six of the students who had answered before him unhesitatingly selected a line that was clearly longer than the comparison line!

The student subject was put in this predicament because, unknown to him, all seven of the other students were not really subjects in the experiment but in league with Asch. They had agreed to answer in prearranged ways on each turn. So on the next card everyone selected a line that was 20 percent too short (4 inches versus 5 inches). On the next card the students all gave the correct answer. But on the next several they mostly gave wrong ones. And when they gave "objectively" wrong ones, they always all agreed on which wrong answer they gave and gave their answers without any hesitation.

Few of the true subjects had any idea that the situation had been rigged. When their turn came around on the rigged trials, three-quarters gave, at least once, the same answer as the majority—the "objectively wrong" answer. A third did so more than half the time.

Yielding was not easy, though. Asch reports that many were "nervous," "confused," "doubt-ridden," and "disoriented." But they went along.

Things were no more comfortable for those who did not go along with the majority; they were often quite ill at ease about disagreeing, saying such things as, "Can't help it" and "I always disagree—darn it." In discussing it with the others immediately after the last card, one of them said, "You're *probably* right, but you *may* be wrong." Then, after the true experiment was explained, this subject said he felt "exulted and relieved." He'd often had the feeling of "to heck with it, I'll go along with the rest" (p. 396). Disagreeing with the majority had been a true ordeal.

Of those who did go along with the rest, in spite of "what they saw with their own eyes," what were their reasons? Most explanations boiled down to these three: (1) the largest number said that although they did not see the lines the same as the majority, they assumed that the majority was correct and that their own perceptions must somehow be wrong; (2) a small number said that although they felt they were completely correct, they did not want to say so because they didn't want to look different to the others; and (3) a few said they actually came to see the line lengths as did the majority.

Social psychologists loved this study. It demonstrated what they had been saying all along: social pressure from the majority can make almost anybody see things their way. Nor did social psychologists mind how much it shocked people. And when people insisted, "I wouldn't go along with something just because other people said it," social psychologists could reply that Asch had gotten these results with normal, intelligent college students. The findings were also substantiated with many other types of people in later experiments.

Nor is being forewarned a sure guarantee. A group of our own students repeated the Asch study with students at Berkeley. They got the usual results, even though several subjects said afterward, in response to the debriefing, "Oh yes, I remember reading about that in psychology!"

One factor does make a difference, causing people to conform even more, and that is the ambiguity of the issue. People will give in more easily about opinions and beliefs than about their direct perceptions. Using a procedure developed by Richard Crutchfield (1955) at the University of California, in which each participant was in a separate booth and saw what they thought were other subjects' answers by way of lights on a control panel, two other Berkeley psychologists (Tuddenham & Macbride, 1959), found that subjects even yielded to agreeing that most Americans eat six meals per day! In a study of military officers (reported in Krech, Crutchfield, & Ballachey, 1962), 37 percent agreed that "I doubt whether I would make a good leader" (although none had agreed to that when asked privately in advance). Most dramatic for the serious point that the social psychologists wanted to make—58 percent of college students were pressured by this procedure into agreeing to the proposition that "Free speech being a privilege rather than a right, it is proper for a society to suspend free speech whenever it feels itself threatened" (p. 509). That would be a majority if it had come to a vote. (Only 19 percent had agreed to the statement when questioned privately in advance.)

Obviously conformity experiments require some heavy-handed deception. When Stanley Milgram, who had worked extensively with Asch, created the ultimate version of these studies, he finally raised the ethical furor that many felt should have come long before.

It was clear that those excited by the Asch and Crutchfield studies had had Nazi Germany in mind—how had all those people agreed to Hitler's horrible plans?[1] The need for an answer to this question was how Milgram rationalized the ordeal he put his subjects through, a demonstration not only of conformity, but of outright obedience to authority, no matter what. Now for the humbling details.

Forty men between twenty and fifty years old were recruited to participate in a study of "memory and learning" at prestigious Yale University via ads in New Haven area newspapers (Milgram, 1963). When a participant arrived, he and what he believed was another subject (actually an accomplice of the experimenter) would draw papers from a hat for the roles of "teacher" or "learner" in an experiment on the role of punishment in learning. It was rigged so that the true subject always became the "teacher"—both papers in the hat said "teacher."

The two of them were then taken into the next room, where the true subject watched as the "learner" was firmly strapped, "to prevent excessive motion," into an "electric chair." Electrode paste was applied "to avoid blisters and burns" and electrodes were attached to the "learner's" wrist. The "learner" had four buttons to press to indicate his response to the learning questions he would be asked.

The "teacher" was then taken to an adjoining room, where he was seated at a very professional looking "shock generator," which had switches on it for generating shocks that went in 15-volt increments from 15 to 450 volts. Each set of three switches had a label above it, ranging from "Slight Shock," through "Strong Shock," all the way up to "Danger: Severe Shock." Finally, over the very last two switches, of 435 and 450 volts, the label just said "XXX." To demonstrate the apparatus and further convince the subject of the reality of the situation, the subject or "teacher" was given a sample shock of 45 volts, using the third switch on the generator.

As you might have guessed, the whole thing was a ruse and the shock generator was not even connected to the electrodes that were fastened to the learner. The sample shock came from a 45-volt battery inside the shock generator. But in virtually every case the subject was quite convinced by the whole thing.

Next each subject was shown how to teach the "learner" a list of word pairs. One pair was to be given at a time and the "learner" had to indicate the correct match from four alternatives, by pressing one of the buttons. The "learner's" choice showed up on a panel on the shock generator. Whenever he made a wrong guess, the "teacher" was supposed to shock him, increasing the shock by 15 volts (one switch) with each wrong guess.

Then the experiment began. The "learner" made some right and some wrong guesses, but missed enough so that the stakes kept getting higher. The "teachers" sweated and laughed nervously, but they kept giving the shocks. If a "teacher" complained, the experimenter instructed him to continue.

The subjects had been told in advance that their small payment was theirs just for showing up. They could keep it no matter what. There was nothing preventing the "teacher" from just getting up and leaving. Yet *every single one of them* continued up to 300 volts, one of the switches marked "intense shock."

At this point the "learner" pounded loudly on the wall, all part of the ruse, and did not give any answer to the test question. The experimenter told the teacher to treat no answer as a wrong answer and to continue. Finally, at this stage, five subjects walked out.

Then at 315 volts, the first switch under "extreme intensity shock," the "learner" again pounded on the wall and again gave no answer. Four more subjects left. But the rest continued. The "learner" was not heard from again.

The "teachers" administering the "shocks" were not taking their job lightly. They would "sweat, tremble, stutter, bite their lips, groan, and dig their fingernails into their flesh" (p. 375). More than a third of them laughed nervously or smiled, and said later it was definitely not because they were enjoying themselves. Three of the "teachers" had "full blown uncontrollable seizures" (p. 375). A forty-six-year-old encyclopedia salesman had a seizure so severe they had to stop the experiment. But the others, twenty-six of the original forty subjects—postal clerks, high school teachers, engineers, salesmen, and the like—continued to the maximum, "XXX" shock of 450 volts.

After the experiment was stopped, to each subject's considerable relief, and after everything was explained to them, Milgram reported that he took care to ensure that the subjects "would leave the experiment in a state of well being" (p. 374). But because the subjects had been so upset by the experience during it, Milgram was violently criticized by many psychologists (for example, Baumrind, 1964) for not stopping this research when he saw the effect it was having.

While other social psychologists believe some of the intensity of this criticism was due to the unpleasantness of the findings, all have taken to heart the ethical questions raised by Milgram's study. Today very few social psychologists would conduct such an experiment, and very few universities would permit them to do so if they tried.

Milgram (1964), however, felt quite justified. The subjects told him they had learned from the experience. A long-term follow-up and examination of subjects by "an independent medical examiner" (a psychiatrist) seemed to confirm this conclusion.

Whatever the rightness or wrongness of Milgram's experiment, it reveals something fundamental about obedience and clearly demonstrates the incredible power of social influence.

Yet another social psychologist has looked at the practical consequences of social pressure. Irving Janis, of Yale University, has systematically analyzed the decision-making processes that led to various major mistakes by U.S. presidents and their advisors (for example, the Bay of Pigs invasion, the Watergate cover-up). What he observed in each case was that decisions were made in a group atmosphere that discouraged dissent, a situation he labeled "groupthink" (Janis, 1972). Everyone wanted to be in harmony with the president and with one another, and their discussions were secret and isolated. Thus the discussants and "advisors" found it very hard to offer an objection based on what they might privately have felt was the wisest course; they found it hard even to evaluate whether they had any independent ideas on the subject.

Other People Influence What We Feel

Stanley Schachter (about whom you learned a little in chapter 1) started one of the most famous sets of studies of social influence by trying to study affiliation (Schachter, 1959). It was already known that people kept in isolation feel anxious, so Schachter wondered if anxious people would prefer to be with one another. And if so, why?

In his first study, when female undergraduates arrived at the laboratory, they were met by the experimenter, a "Dr. Gregor Zillstein" (first played by Schachter, but later by various graduate students), who informed each subject that he was sorry, but the needs of science required that the experiment would involve some strong electric shocks—but not to worry, "There would be no permanent damage." The room was full of apparatus, and it all seemed very believable.

Then the student was told that while the experiment was being set up, she could wait in another room. Offhandedly Zillstein explained that she could either wait alone or with another female student who was also waiting to be in the experiment. The subjects' choice of where to wait was the true purpose of the experiment. After the choice was made the subject was "debriefed," and no doubt much relieved.[2]

Schachter found that under these conditions misery loves company. But the next question was, why did the subjects choose to wait with others? There were two theories: (1) distraction and (2) the need to be with someone to help figure out what you are feeling. So, he did a second experiment. In this version, some of the subjects were given the option of waiting either alone or with another student waiting for the same experiment; others were given the option of waiting alone or with students waiting to see their faculty advisers. Theory 1 predicted more choices to wait with another young woman who was waiting for her adviser (she would offer more distraction). Theory 2 predicted more choices to wait with another young woman waiting for the same experiment (so they could verbally or nonverbally compare what they were feeling). The results unambiguously supported theory 2. In fact, not one of the subjects wanted to wait with the student waiting to see her advisor!

From this finding, it occurred to Schachter and Jerry Singer, his student at the time, that people probably often use social information to determine what they feel, particularly when what they ought to feel in a situation is not completely clear from objective information. This general idea had been formalized earlier, in reference to self-evaluations of abilities and attitudes, under the name "social comparison theory" (Festinger, 1954). (John Arrowood wrote in 1978 that social comparison is "everyone's second favorite theory," the first being whatever fashionable topic they are working on at the moment.)

Schachter and Singer (1962) suggested that since those studying emotion had not identified clearly different physiological states for different emotions, that perhaps emotions arise as a combination of a generalized physiological state of being "stirred up" (arousal of the sympathetic nervous system, to be precise) along with a mental interpretation of that state. Or as they put it, "The cognition, in a sense, exerts a steering function" (p. 380).

To test this idea, they set up the following experiment. Male introductory psychology students who had volunteered to participate (and whose medical records had been checked by the university health service to be sure the experiment was safe for them), were told they were taking part in a study of the effects on vision of a new vitamin, "suproxin." One at a time the subjects were given an injection. For most of the subjects it was actually a shot of adrenalin, a hormone which creates physiological effects like those associated with emotion—including the subjectively noticeable changes of "palpitation, tremor, and sometimes a feeling of flushing and accelerated breathing" (p. 382). About 30 percent of the subjects, as a control condition, were given an injection which contained only saline solution, which has no physiological effect at all.

After receiving their shots of, supposedly, "suproxin," some subjects were told that the fictitious drug created "side effects" such as trembling hands—all the effects known to be produced by adrenalin. Another group was told to expect side effects that in fact would be very unlikely to occur from adrenalin (such as itching and numb feet). Finally, one group was told that the "suproxin" was "mild and harmless and would have no side effects" (p. 382). The group who received the saline solution was also given this last speech.

Thus, there were four groups. Of those receiving adrenalin, some expected the actual effects adrenalin produces, some expected effects that adrenalin never produces, and some expected no side effects. Those who received the saline solution also expected no side effects. The idea was that those who had a proper explanation for their arousal would be unaffected by anything that subsequently happened to them, while those who did not have any good explanation for an onset of arousal, would look to their circumstances for an explanation and manifest an emotion appropriate to those circumstances.

Schachter had pretested the adrenalin injections on his graduate students (an experience well remembered by his victims). He knew that the effect of the size of injection they were giving would be clearly noticed by most subjects about three to five minutes after the injection. Thus, for the subjects to associate the onset of the physiological symptoms with the circumstances, the circumstances had to be created quickly. So, immediately after the injection, the experimenter brought in another "subject," who was introduced as having just received the same injection. But actually he was a confederate of the experimenter.[3] The two were then asked to wait in this room for twenty minutes while the "vitamin" took effect.

At this point half the subjects began what was called the "anger condition." They were asked to complete a questionnaire while they waited, a questionnaire especially designed to create annoyance. In addition, the experimenter's confederate did everything he could to act annoyed about it. In fact, before even looking at the questionnaire, the confederate started complaining about the experiment. He also paced himself to complete items at the same rate as the true subject, complaining about each item: "Boy this is a long one," or "Look at question 9—how ridiculous can you get?", or "That's a real insult."

In fact, there was much to complain about. The first questions were innocuous enough, but personal questions soon followed, like "What is your father's income?" Then came insulting questions, asking the respondents to identify the member of their families, for whom it was most true that he or she "does not bathe or wash regularly" or "seems to need psychiatric care." "None" was not a choice; one member of the family had to be listed.

At about this point the bogus subject ripped up the questionnaire and stamped out of the room. If the actual subject continued with the questionnaire on his own, he faced increasingly insulting items. The last asked, "With how many men (other than your father) has your mother had extramarital relationships?" The lowest multiple-choice answer was "4 and under." Subjects were steaming.

The other half of the subjects participated in what was called the "euphoria condition."[4] In this condition when the experimenter left the true subject and the bogus subject in the room together, there was no questionnaire to fill out. Instead they were told that while they were waiting they could make use of any rubber bands, paper, or anything else in the room.

Immediately the experimenter's confederate started doodling. Then he crumpled up his paper and started playing basketball with it and the wastebasket, making comments such as "two points" and "the old jump shot is really on today." If the true subject did not join in spontaneously, he was invited to.

Next the confederate started making paper airplanes; then a slingshot; then he located an old hula hoop and played with it. All the while he was the essence of friendliness, inviting the subject to join in the fun.

Throughout the "waiting period" the subjects were being watched through a one-way mirror and the extent of their participation was being recorded. Of course, the procedure was double blind: neither the confederate nor the raters were allowed to know what injection and what information the subject had received.

Following their wait and before the expected eye test, the subjects completed some questionnaires on various topics. Buried among them were a couple questions on their current mood.

The results were a bit complicated.[5] But the overall result was quite clear: those who got adrenalin and had been told to expect the adrenalin effects as side effects showed very little emotion. They did not join in much with the confederates and they did not show much mood change in the final questionnaire. Similarly, those who got the saline solution and were not physiologically aroused also showed little emotion, either in their behavior or on the questionnaire. Subjects in these conditions often just sat there while the confederate went through his bizarre antics.

But those who were aroused and did not have any explanation for their symptoms, or who had been given the wrong explanation, strongly showed the emotion of the condition they were in. In fact, in the euphoria condition, one subject "threw open the window and, laughing, hurled paper basketballs at passersby." Another "jumped on the table and spun one hula hoop on his leg and the other on his neck."

Jerry Singer remembers this as an experiment that was both fun to do and that felt important, scientifically, to be doing.

The ability to see people being manipulated into one or another emotion simply on the basis of what a model was doing was such a striking demonstration of behavior. And the ability of this nonspecific drug to bring it about just seemed a source of wonder. We of course didn't know how well it was working until it was all over. But it was an interesting study to run—for the first 20 or so subjects. I must confess that having run all of them, by the time you get to the 175th subject, some of that wonder has dissipated.

Other People Influence What We *Are*

Social psychologist Robert Rosenthal (Rosenthal & Fode, 1963) at Harvard started out studying social influence in an odd way—by randomly assigning rats of the same strain to two groups of students, who were to teach the rats to run a maze. One group of students was told that they had bright rats, the other that they had dull ones. The allegedly "bright" rats were consistently better at learning to run mazes, apparently because, according to questionnaires, the students found these rats more "likable," so they handled them quite differently.

Fascinated by these results, Rosenthal and Lenore Jacobson (1968) did the same study in a classroom, telling elementary school teachers that they had certain students in their classes who were "academic spurters." In fact, these students were selected at random. Absolutely nothing else was done by the researchers to single out these children. Yet by the end of the school year, 30 percent of the children arbitrarily named as spurters had gained an average of 22 IQ points, and almost all had gained at least 10 IQ points. The "spurters" were also rated much higher in their classroom performance by their teachers. Rosenthal compared his results to an expensive "total push" campaign funded by the Title I education act that led, after three years, to gains that were much smaller than even the gains for the control students in these classrooms. Something had definitely happened to the teachers of these students.

Rosenthal was fairly certain the teachers did not spend more time with the alleged "spurters" because these students improved less on their verbal scores than their reasoning scores. Rather, he thinks the teachers were more excited about teaching these students, and maybe about teaching generally. And they must have subtly communicated respect for and enthusiasm about these students, so that the students themselves felt more capable of understanding and anticipated better performance from themselves. Rosenthal calls this the Pygmalion effect. Others call it the Rosenthal effect. And still others see it as a special case of what has come to be called "self-fulfilling prophecy."

Social psychologists love studies that demonstrate how much social influences determine a person's self-image. A recent favorite (1977) was conducted by Mark Snyder, Beth Tanke, and Ellen Berscheid at the University of Minnesota, some years after the "Dr. Zillstein" era. At the time, Berscheid was researching interpersonal attraction and Snyder was studying the effects of self-fulfilling prophecy. Thus it was natural for them, together with their graduate student at that time, Tanke, to design an experiment to look at self-fulfilling prophecy in the area of attractiveness.

It was a quite complicated experiment to carry out (as Tanke put it, "in the grand tradition" of Asch, Schachter, etc.), involving considerable staging and management of when and where subjects would show up. But the basic idea was simple. Male and female students participated in a study described to them as on "the processes by which people become acquainted with each other" (p. 659). A male and a female subject would arrive separately, and then hold a ten-minute, get-acquainted "phone conversation" through earphones and microphone. The conversation was tape recorded. The male subject was also given what he thought was a picture of the female subject.

Half the young men were randomly chosen to receive a picture of a young woman, not the experimental partner, who had been independently judged to be attractive, and half a picture of a young woman who had been independently judged to be unattractive.[6] After the experiment, it was no surprise that independent judges, listening to recordings of only the male subject's part of the conversation, could easily pick out which young men were talking to an "attractive" and which to an "unattractive" young woman. What was more surprising was that, when listening to only the female subject's half of the conversation, other male college students rated as more attractive those women who had been talking to a male subject who thought he was talking to an attractive woman! In other words, however attractive a woman may be, she sounds much more attractive to men when she is talking with a man who is responding to her as if she is attractive.

The Reasons Social Psychologists Emphasize
Social Influence

Although almost every social psychologist considers it important to demonstrate the impact of social influences, their reasons vary a bit. Some seem simply to want to wipe the clouds of illusion from our eyes. It was once said that humanity received three great blows to its self-esteem: that the earth was not at the center of the universe (Copernicus' doing); that humans had evolved from animals (Darwin's blow); and, thanks to Freud, that "rationality" and "civilization" are a cover-up for unconscious, irrational instincts. Social psychologists seem to want to add a fourth: that most of our "individual acts of free will" are guided almost exclusively by situational and social influences.

Besides just bursting a bubble, most social psychologists hope this insight will help people to take social influences into account. At least, as Berscheid put it in our interview with her, one might tend "to be less hard on other people and also less self-congratulatory about one's own accomplishments or good qualities" when one knows the real source of most behavior. Social psychologist Russ Fazio said something similar to us: with an appreciation of social influence, people "shouldn't have such a blaming-the-victim mentality."

But most social psychologists hope to have a far greater effect on the human race: to help people resist social pressures to conform to evil. The rise of Naziism in Germany and then the rise of McCarthyism in the United States had a profound effect on many psychologists. Some, like Lewin, had fled Hitler, and nearly all the rest were students of someone who had. As we have said, they felt compelled to prove that "it *can* happen here," or anywhere, if the social pressure is strong enough.

Other social psychologists think that most individuals probably cannot resist social influences, but that individuals can affect what those social influences are. Lewin is said to have stated, "No change in attitude without a change in culture, no change in culture without a change in attitude." In other words, we can at least manage social influence by choosing the company we keep. If we want to be compassionate, we associate with unselfish, dedicated types. If we want to be logical, we hang out with logicians.

On a larger scale, we can change society by seeing that institutions such as schools, the media, and government provide the "right social influences" for good citizenship. Often these institutions do not recognize, or do not want to recognize, their crucial role. Or it may be too hard for institutions to change, once again because their members are under social pressure not to deviate. All this makes the social psychologist unpopular sometimes. It is easier, even nicer, to leave the solution of social problems to the individual. Berscheid commented:

> I think many times governments and established institutions do not like the nature of our answers, because very frequently our answers are that your problem is not the people, but the context in which these people are living, working, and operating. You cannot blame them. Their behavior is a product of their nature interacting with this context. A lot of institutions (including universities) don't want to hear this, because they don't want the responsibility to make the kinds of changes that would bring about, for example, improved job performance, reduced violence, or fewer divorces. In not blaming the individual, we take a different approach. But it is a vital one. As a result, I think we are not the darling of the social and behavioral sciences—we are not even the darling of psychology—and I think tomorrow belongs to us.

Individuals' Influences on Society

In spite of their crusade, social psychologists admit that individuals do influence society too. They have to admit it, because they have influenced society so often themselves. And as we have said, many believe the purpose of their crusade is to show that one must strive to be independent, which implies that one can be. Asch, when introducing his group pressure studies, always explains that he is studying the factors that make people resist group pressure as well as the factors that make them yield to it. Other social psychologists have also emphasized that with greater knowledge of the process of social influence, individuals can and do have a greater impact, whether they write advertising copy, teach students, run for office, rear children, or manage personnel.

But a duel among skilled influencers still leaves some people pawns. On the final page of the most influential social psychology textbook of the early 1960s, Krech, et al. (1962) said that "the critical problem toward which all the behavioral sciences must be directed is how man can remain an *individual in society*" (p. 529).

Perhaps the answer comes not from the research but from the lives of social psychologists. By their very work they demonstrate that every change in society still must come, finally, out of the brain of single individuals, thinking in their wonderfully idiosyncratic ways.

The next chapter continues this theme of social psychologists' insistence on the power of social influence. We show that this stubborn insistence has led them to a less known but far more controversial stance: that *the social group*, the source of social influence, is not just a term for a collection of people, but is an utterly real entity with a life of its own, independent of its members.

Notes

1. Dorwin Cartwright (1979) went so far as to say that the single person who had the most impact on social psychology was Adolf Hitler. It is easy to see why. Hitler lived at the time when social psychology took shape and drove many of its leading scholars, who had been scattered around Europe, to the East Coast of the United States. There they huddled together, angry and confused, and went to work on the task of getting even, or at least getting clearer about what had happened in Germany. Hitler raised questions about humanity's weakness in the face of social pressure that society wanted answered and was willing to support social psychologists to study. He was also the cause of a war effort in the United States that brought leading psychologists together to work for the first time, with ample funds, on practical social problems.

2. No one ever received any actual shocks in this experiment. However, at an informal get-together of former University of Minnesota social psychology students not long ago, a recent graduate told how that old dentist's-chair-turned-"shock-chair" that Schachter had used to help scare his subjects was still kept as a revered memento, twenty-five years later. At that point the older social psychologists present, who had been Schachter's assistants on that study, looked blankly at one another and finally reported to the disillusioned recent graduates that Schachter had never used such a chair in that study!

3. One of the two confederates in this study was Bibb Latane—a tall, lanky, red-haired, young student of Schachter's at the time—but whom you will remember from chapter 1 as the senior researcher in the bystander-apathy study. It is said that he should have got an award for the performance we are about to describe.

4. Actually, approximately four-sevenths were in the euphoria condition. Half of each group that expected some side effect was in each emotion condition, except that all of the group that expected irrelevant side effects were in the euphoria condition.

5. Basically, the problem was that some of those who got adrenalin did not become

physiologically aroused, some of those who got saline did become aroused, and some of those who got adrenalin and were told to expect no side effects did in fact attribute their arousal to the injection. If, however, on the basis of various measures of these things, one eliminates subjects who fell into these three categories of responses inappropriate to instructions, the results reported here hold up quite nicely. Schachter and Singer also report several other studies which confirm their result. The variation was probably largely due to the injection itself. They did consider some alternatives to the injection procedure that might have obviated these problems (for example "ventilating the experimental room with vaporized adrenalin"), but these were not practical.

6. Getting photographs of unattractive young women was not easy. Tanke explained that you cannot simply go up to someone and ask for her picture for the "unattractive condition in an experiment." The researchers first tried a modeling agency, reasoning the models could make themselves look unattractive with makeup and so forth. The first modeling agency they approached asked if they wanted the models "dressed or undressed." The second modeling agency understood the idea a little better, but the models had such attractive features that all they could do with makeup was look beat up and tired, which was not the idea. Finally, the researchers asked some ordinary young women from a neighboring college to "make themselves unattractive" and be photographed for $10. The students had a good time grooming themselves for the part, did not mind because no one at the University of Minnesota knew them anyway, and the researchers got their needed photos.

3

"It's a Good Group—I Just Don't Like the People in It."

BECAUSE the point we made about social psychologists in the last chapter is so true, we are going to continue with it, but take it one step further: for social psychologists, social influence is not just important—it is *real*, and it comes from a real entity, the social group.

Of course, to most people *real* means what you can touch or see or bump against. And it is true, as one of the first American social psychologists, Floyd Allport, liked to say, "You can't stumble over a group" (quoted in Deaux and Wrightsman, 1984, p. 360). But social psychologists do not dwell much on metaphysical speculation of what is ultimately real. They have a very practical definition of reality: "Whatever has effects is real." Remember when you were a skin cell back at the start of the last chapter? You knew your life was influenced by the activities of all the other cells as a whole. Their influence was real. In fact, it was so real that, if as a cell you could think, you probably would have had a name for all the other cells as a whole—perhaps "the body." In the same way, you as a human have names for the assemblages of humans you call family, city, government, or psychology class. Not only do you have names for them, but you probably think about them as if they were real and can affect you.

A few social psychologists like Allport hold out that a social "body" is nothing but a lot of cells, or individuals, assembled in one place. But the majority look at a group of individuals communicating together as a whole that is something more than an assemblage of parts. In this chapter we want to look at the history of why social psychologists have come to look at social groups as real—and why it matters so much to them, and seems so natural.

Once Again, Lewin

This emphasis comes, according to Berscheid, "directly from Kurt Lewin." She points out that in Lewin's time psychology was very individualistic and it was very important to Lewin to change that direction, "for us to carry that torch . . . against the Cartesian-Newtonian view of the world." That world view was of a machine wherein A hits B and B moves C and C shoves D up against E. In physics, these were the laws of classical mechanics; in psychology, they were the laws governing the association of mental elements, and then later, stimuli and responses.

But in physics, just after the turn of the century, and just after physics thought it knew just about all there was to know, the whole structure of physics started to unravel. Everything about those classical laws began to be proven wrong when they were taken to their extremes. That is, those laws were not obeyed by either subatomic particles or objects light years away.

Quantum field theory was the result, a theory which says everything is connected to everything else through nonmaterial but utterly real fields. In our example, when A moves, the influence of that move is felt as vibrations in a field of which B, C, D, and E are all part. The important object of study is not A, B, C, D, or E, or the contact between any pair, but the field in which they are embedded as interdependent parts.

Similar developments occurred in mathematics and chemistry, such that fields were the new and necessary concept of the day. It was this "field theory" approach that Lewin wished to bring to psychology. He saw that psychology was still trying to imitate the old, classical, physical science laws, while the physical sciences themselves had seen the limited usefulness of those laws several decades before.

For example, Lewin wrote:

> Groups are sociological wholes; the unity of these sociological wholes can be defined . . . in the same way as a unity of any other dynamic whole, namely, by the interdependence of its parts. Such a definition takes mysticism out of the group conception and brings the problems

down to a thoroughly . . . testable basis. . . . It means a full recognition of the fact that properties of a social group, such as its organization . . . its goals, are something different from the organization . . . and the goals of the individuals in it. (1948, pp. 72–73)

Lewin established a Research Center for Group Dynamics at the Massachusetts Institute of Technology immediately after World War II. This center began a tradition of research on groups that dominated social psychology through the 1950s and continues to play a major role in the field. A typical study in this tradition compared the productivity of groups when they are organized into different communication patterns, or looked at how groups treat deviants, or distinguished the different types of leaders that spontaneously emerge during group interaction.

The unique contribution of this approach is apparent in each of these studies: they could never have even been conceived without thinking of a group as more than just a collection of individuals. These are studies of *group* productivity, *group* patterns of communication, *group* reactions to deviance, *group* roles. The patterns and processes seen in these studies have little to do with the particular personalities or histories of the people in the groups. Often they do not even have much to do with how many people are in the group. They are processes that are properties of groups, not of the individuals in the groups.

Of Risks and Norms

Let's look in greater detail at some studies which grew out of the assumption that groups are real—and also demonstrate that reality. Most of the experiments chosen for discussion in this section were not directly influenced by Lewin or the MIT Research Center for Group Dynamics, which allows us to point out that this way of thinking did not originate exclusively with Lewin, but was characteristic of everyone in the field—almost. (We'll come soon to the "almost": Floyd Allport.)

One series of studies (reviewed in Myers, 1982) focuses on what has come to be called *group polarization*. Typically, individuals are presented with a situation which requires a decision or the giving of some advice. First they privately indicate their personal decision or advice along a scale from, for example, "Do it only if it's absolutely safe" to "Do it no matter what." Then they meet with several others to discuss the situation and perhaps come to a decision. Next they are each asked again, privately and individually, for their decision on the advice to give. In almost every such study, the average of the private decisions has been found to have changed following group discussion, and consistently it is a more extreme version of whatever was the average of the group members' advice before the discussion. In other words, the individuals are influenced to develop more socially typical attitudes.

A group of five individuals might be told about a talented writer named Henry who has been writing cheap westerns to make a living. He now has an idea for a great novel. But if it is not successful, he will have wasted several years. The individuals in the group check one of several answers indicating their advice, ranging from "Henry should attempt to write the novel if the chances are at least . . . 1 in 10 that the novel will be a success," all the way to ". . . only if it is certain (i.e., 10 in 10) that the novel will be a success" (Myers, 1982, p. 126).

After indicating their decision individually, the group members meet and discuss Henry's situation. Finally, the group may be asked to come to a joint decision, and then the individuals' give their private judgments after the discussion. In Henry's case, before the group discussion people usually advise him to risk the novel even if the odds are somewhat against him. So after the discussion, they say he should "go for it" against even longer odds. That is, the *average of private decisions*, after discussion, changes to become more extreme in the same direction.

This phenomenon was originally of interest because it seemed to show that groups make riskier decisions than individuals. It was a surprising result, with what looked like interesting implications for business, government, and the like. The phenomenon was dubbed the "shift to risk" or "risky shift" effect. However subsequent research showed that the risky choices were due to using tasks where most people would make a fairly risky choice to begin with. When the decision involves an outcome which most people would advise others to avoid unless the odds against it are very high—for example, doing something that could injure innocent parties—one sees a "conservative shift."

Another series of studies illustrates the independence of group norms from the individuals that make up the group. This research began years ago (in 1935) with a study of Muzafer Sherif, who also did the Robber's Cave study described in chapter 1. Sherif made use of what is known as the *autokinetic effect*. This is the illusion of movement of a small point of light in a completely dark room (an effect originally discovered in astronomy). This nonexistent movement is seen by virtually everyone put in the situation, even if they are aware of the effect. In fact, Sherif reports that it is so strong that if you put people in a room on chairs without back support, some will lose their bearings and practically fall off their chairs when shown the point of light.

The phenomenon was useful to Sherif because there is no objective answer to how far the point of light moves, since it in fact never moves. Thus he could ask subjects to view a number of such points of light, one after the other, and make judgments for each as to how far the dot had moved. Doing this, he found that people tend to make their judgments within a certain range. Once the range is established, they tend to make subsequent decisions within that range.

For his experiment on norms, Sherif had subjects look at the same light in pairs and in groups of three. After each viewing, each subject was asked to say how far the point moved. The result was clear: the groups developed a joint, group standard—or *norm*—as to the range and average distance of movements. Even when those individuals were later tested alone, on a different day, their judgments reflected the norm they had established in the group. In fact, a later study (Bovard, 1948) found that the norms affected the individuals when tested twenty-eight days later; and other researchers (Rohrer, Baron, Hoffman, & Swander, 1954) found the effect a year later.

These experiments led to a new series of studies, beginning in the 1960s. Robert Jacobs and Donald Campbell (1961) of Northwestern University wanted to see what would happen to a group norm if the members of the group were changed one at a time. They saw this as most similar to the situation in society, where traditions are maintained over generations, even though all the people in a society are eventually new.

In their Sherif-style autokinetic-effect experiment, groups of two, three, or four were shown the point of light thirty times. Then one of the members would leave and a new member would join for the next thirty times. Then again, an old member would leave and a new member join. Thus in groups of two, after two times through, the whole group was new; groups of three were new after three times through; groups of four, after four times through.

In this study, groups typically started out with a mean of about 3.8 inches of movement, if left to themselves. But Jacobs and Campbell were interested in the maintenance of "arbitrary norms." So they privately arranged to have some of the original group act as their confederates and suggest that they saw a movement of 15 to 16 inches. They arranged the seating so that these confederates always spoke first in the first group of thirty viewings. This procedure established group norms which averaged 15.8 inches, a classic conformity result. But more important, "Significant remnants of the culture persisted for four or five generations beyond the last [confederate]. . . . Gradually . . . the arbitrary norm decayed and the group judgments drifted away from it back to the natural norm found in the control groups." (p. 657) In every case some significant effect of the original norm was maintained well beyond when the last subject who had been exposed to the confederates had left the group.

Being social psychologists, Jacobs and Campbell were not very impressed with this outcome. They had hypothesized that cultures would maintain social norms indefinitely, and had hoped to show that even an arbitrary, useless norm would continue over many generations. Later M.K. MacNeil (reported in Sherif & Sherif, 1969) found that if the norm was not set by the confederates to be quite so extreme, a group norm is maintained much longer. But even so, there was a clear tendency for the "arbitrary" norm to revert to "reality" as the generations progressed.

Ten years later Karl Weick and David Gilfillan (1971) at the University of Minnesota repeated the experiment with one very important modification. Instead of using autokinetic effect judgments (for which there seems to be a "natural" judgment after all), groups played a "common target game." In this game, three people independently gave numbers which they were supposed to be trying to make add up to a total they'd been given as a goal. The groups could use different strategies: two easy ones, which groups would typically develop on their own, and two difficult-to-use strategies which, though equally effective, were not usually spontaneously developed. At the start, one set of groups was given an easy strategy to use if they chose. The other groups were given a hard strategy. The rest of the experiment was much like the Jacobs and Campbell study, with new persons rotating in and an old person leaving after every twenty-four tries at the game.

Weick and Gilfillan found that the hard strategy only maintained itself, on the average, as long as one of the members of the original group was in the group. After that, most groups spontaneously adopted one of the two easier strategies. This was roughly consistent with what Campbell and Jacobs had found for the arbitrary auto-kinetic norms. But for the groups initially given an easy strategy, they maintained that particular easy strategy, with no decline in its use, for the full eleven generations of the study.

As we said, experiments like these on group norms both assumed and demonstrated the reality of groups and their independence of the characteristics of the members. Where did this certainty about the reality of groups come from?

A Taste for *Quasselstrippe*

When you like something, you probably tend to argue for its reality. Social psychologists, even more than most scientists, seem to like groups. They like to work in groups, to play in groups, and to study groups. While interviewing social psychologists for this book, we often asked how their ideas were developed. Again and again we heard, "I don't know how we came up with the idea. We were talking and . . ."

The "we" was usually a few professors and a few graduate students, working together. When asked about how they gathered to meet—in regular seminars, or lunch meetings, or whatever—the usual response was surprise. Things just worked that way. Everyone was always interacting and thinking as a group.

All the sciences seem to require more of a group effort these days. In fact, life is so complex that almost everything has to be done by teamwork. It is harder and harder to identify the one Great Mind responsible for some idea, be it the computer or the Big Bang Theory, or the design of the clothes you are wearing. Frequently in science, however, the team is composed of an authority surrounded by a lot of disciples.

In contrast, in social psychology we get the impression that colleagues tend to collaborate more. Even when students do work with a mentor, it is more often on a relatively equal footing. This seems to be as much for the pleasure of having company as it is to generate better ideas and distribute the workload.

Our impression was corroborated by social psychologist Marilyn Brewer. When we asked her whether there was anything that distinguishes social psychologists from other psychologists, she said quite spontaneously, "Yes. They're more social! They tend to form a more cohesive group within a psychology department than other specialties of psychology."

Is this another Lewinian legacy? Certainly Lewin worked this way. Nearly every development of his emerged in a group setting. He inspired group thinking, and it inspired him. Fritz Heider, a long-time friend of Lewin's, recounts that whenever Heider would suggest that he and Lewin get together with someone Heider wanted to introduce to Lewin, "characteristically he thought at once of a larger gathering" (1983, p. 88).

Lewin's informal group meetings in Berlin, his *Quasselstrippe*, continued even amid the cornfields of Iowa. His students and colleagues in the American Midwest translated *Quasselstrippe* as "the Hot-Air Club." Instead of Berlin's Schwedisch Cafe, they met in Iowa City's Round Window Restaurant, where the owner let them use an upstairs room to eat their bag lunches, so long as they bought coffee or tea. The lunch meetings were full of "animated conversation, bad puns, and much laughter . . . with Lewin joining in the fun as much as anyone" (Marrow, 1969, p. 82). In such an atmosphere of group creativity, who could doubt the reality and centrality of group life?

According to several of the people we interviewed, the creation of this democratic and intellectually impassioned atmosphere was an explicit goal of many of Lewin's students when they became leading figures in their own right. For example, Leon Festinger (Lewin's most famous student, about whom you will learn more in chapter 7) met regularly with his students at Stanford University over lunch and had them over to his house often. And Schachter's students at the University of Minnesota seemed to be constantly meeting in a group. Peals of laughter would emanate from any room they were in. The favorite game seemed to be, "Can you top this idea?" Not a bad game for scientists to play, but so much easier in a convivial atmosphere.

Other Reasons Social Psychologists See Groups as Real

Besides loving to work in groups, social psychologists probably treat groups as real for several other reasons. Jerry Singer (of the team Schachter and Singer, whose work was described in the preceding chapter) suggests that the emphasis on the reality of the social may arise from social psychologists' experience of manipulating social variables in the laboratory and seeing their powerful effects first hand. And Lee Ross (another former student of Schachter's, who is discussed in the next chapter) suggests the reason may be that social psychologists have a language for describing groups. It is hard to treat something as real if you do not know many words that describe its qualities or what it does.

Nor should we overemphasize Lewin's role at the expense of others, especially Sherif and Newcomb. These two studied with Gardner Murphy, and Murphy also very much emphasized the group reality. Newcomb held that groups are just "as real and ineluctable as intraindividual determinants of behavior" (1974, p. 379). And the Sherifs noted that "collective action of a group has properties peculiar to itself" (1973, p. 8). No doubt it is natural for almost anyone studying social phenomena to think of groups as real. Almost anyone.

Floyd Allport—A Shy Social Psychologist (There Had To Be One)

There was one major critic of the idea that groups are real—Floyd Allport. Today he is often confused with his brother Gordon. But while they were active, in the 1920s to 1960s, no one who knew them confused them. Gordon was humorous and outgoing, Floyd was serious and reclusive. Gordon's specialty was personality, and Floyd's of course was social psychology. But while Gordon and Floyd claimed to disagree good-naturedly on most scientific assumptions and conclusions, they both held to a strong emphasis on the individual and, implicitly, individualism.

Perhaps this came from their upbringing by two people who seemed to have been strong individuals themselves—a father who had been a businessman until midlife, then became a country doctor, and a mother who was both a free-thinking Midwestern school teacher and a pious daughter of a founder of the Free Methodist Church (who later became "liberal, philosophical, and even critical" of its theology; F. Allport, 1974, p. 3).

Or perhaps, for Floyd, this insistence on the individual in the face of the prevailing norms in social psychology came from a natural shyness and stubbornness. Floyd himself admits that he "did not mingle much with colleagues and associates." He also "accepted nothing on faith," but subjected everything to "excruciating logic" to "the bitter end." Thus, Floyd had not actually experienced the reality of group life to the degree others did, and he was not one to go along with an idea just because it was popular.

His major research was on something called *social facilitation*. What is generally considered to be "the first social psychology experiment" was done on this topic—in 1898, by Triplett. Triplett found that individuals wound fish wire faster when they were in a group than when they were alone. Exciting research, yes? But Allport extended the approach in various, actually interesting ways, so that social facilitation remains an important topic in social psychology.

Social facilitation, however, has always been a study of how an individual is affected by being in the presence of other people. This research, and all research done by Floyd Allport, never required that one think of the group as an entity, but only as a situation. Allport condemned what he called "the group fallacy":

> Nationality, Free-masonry, Catholicism, and the like are not group minds. . . . they are sets of ideals, thoughts, and habits repeated in each individual mind and existing only in those minds. . . . All theories which partake of the group fallacy have the unfortunate consequence of diverting attention from the locus of cause and effect, namely, the behavior mechanism of the individual. (1924, p. 9)

The Vision Remains

In spite of Allport, the group-is-real position has largely prevailed in social psychology. (In fact, eventually even he modified his position a little.) What we have been trying to demonstrate in this chapter is that this position seems to remain not so much by virtue of any formal research or philosophical analysis, or by virtue of the prestige of its adherents, but because if you are studying social life, it generally just makes sense to think of social groups as real. Social psychologists see the world that way. Why? Either because people aware of social realities become social psychologists, or because their social psychology training gives them that perspective. Either way, in the next chapter we will explore how this vision affects the personal life of social psychologists and how, at least in part, they probably come by this vision.

4

"Here's Your Hat. What's Your Hurry?"

WHILE attending a psychology convention not long ago, one of us was introduced to a fellow social psychologist. We spent several minutes getting acquainted in the usual way for two academics. That is, we played a little duet of simultaneously trying to make an impression on the other while trying to form one. We busily exchanged information about our status, not very subtly letting each other know where we'd got our degrees, whom we'd studied with, what we'd published. And we measured each other's intellectual sharpness and wit, and searched out each other's potential for stimulation and personal warmth. We even followed the usual path for any two strangers meeting—slowly, very carefully, revealing something personal about ourselves, and then when the other reciprocates, revealing a little more. All the while, as the conversation progressed, the space between us and our postures adjusted to the growing easiness and informality of the relationship—though we were also both feeling rushed by the nature of the setting. After all, it would have been improper to have extended the conversation very long under the norms for meeting people at conferences, where everyone has many professional and personal appointments to keep and sessions to attend.

Social psychologists have studied the process of getting acquainted in some detail, and the encounter just described is probably as typical of a meeting of two mathematicians or two plumbers. But in this case, when two social psychologists were meeting, there was yet another element: we were both very conscious of what was going on between us. I *knew*, immediately, when I was showing off some symbol of professional status. I *knew*, immediately, when she was testing my sharpness. And—this is what made it most interesting— we each knew the other knew, and each knew the other knew the other knew!

Of course, this knowledge didn't change anything about what we did. Neither of us was so sure we knew what was going on that we were willing to risk the embarrassment of verbalizing it. Anyway, it was fun to be watching the game we were playing.

Artists see more in a sunset than other people, and physicists see more in the shape of the ocean's waves than the rest of us. The specialty of social psychology is the relationships between people— issues such as how people talk to one another, how they achieve status and power, how they become attracted to each other, and how they show one another their feelings and beliefs. Thus it is not surprising that two social psychologists would notice these phenomena in their daily lives. Just as a botanist can recognize dozens of different plants where we might see "a field of green stuff," the social psychologist recognizes dozens of different ways people relate.

This recognition can make a social psychologist's life different. Much richer. He or she perceives subtleties that others miss. In this chapter we want to elaborate on how it feels to have this much social awareness, describe some of its sources, and then see what its fruits have been in terms of research and insights that have been shared with the rest of society.

In the Hall of Mirrors

Recently we asked a few social psychologists about their impressions of what goes on at the annual cocktail party of the Division of Personality and Social Psychology at the American Psychological Association Convention held each August. All of them said something like "Oh, it's the usual thing" and then proceeded, without a second thought, to give an intricate and sophisticated description of the patterns and processes going on at that party. Never did they comment on the actual content of what was said or who was there. Nothing so mundane as that. Spontaneously their description was of the social dynamics.

Similarly, Strickland, Aboud, and Gergen (1976) reprinted a transcript of the last session of an international meeting of social psychologists in Canada, at which some of the graduate students who were attending brought up what they saw as the domination of the field by the older, more established members. This led to a lively discussion about the social structure of the field, then the social structure of the current meeting, and then the structure and dynamics of the conversation, and finally they started discussing why the structure and dynamics of the conversation was the subject of the conversation!

Life for social psychologists is not always a hall of mirrors of social dynamics. Nor are they always able to use this increased awareness of social realities to any great advantage in their personal lives. They can be wallflowers at a party, just like anyone else. But at least they can entertain themselves by analyzing what everyone else is doing, and maybe using it to come up with a great research idea.

Above all, social psychologists are used to turning off their observational powers around nonpsychologists, who tend anyway to say things like, "Oh, you're a psychologist. I'd better watch what I say." Even with their colleagues they are often too busy discussing new ideas to pay attention to the process underlying the discussion. But one can be aware without giving attention to something, and it is probably safe to say that this subtle awareness of the social reality never really leaves most social psychologists.

We asked a number of them about this social awareness. Maybe the best answer was from Ted Sarbin, a major figure famous for, among other things, his iconoclastic applications of role theory (for example, that mental illness and hypnotic trances are both learned roles). He was emphatic when we asked him if he was aware of social interaction processes.

> Oh yes. Especially since I've gotten into the analysis of context. I see people interacting, living out their life stories. I sit back and ask myself what's his or her life story and in what way are we contributing to that development. I look at people humanely, but I can't help but see the social psychological variables.

From our own experience, if we are sitting at dinner with a few friends, the lines of attraction or annoyance, the patterns of status and power, the connections of mutual interest—these seem as real as if they were strands strung between people, creating a social net. It is not that we necessarily think about these ties. They are simply there, spontaneously, in the same way that a fashion designer is spontaneously aware of the clothes people wear—of the fabric, cut, and colors—even when he or she is discussing other things.

What is the source of this fine-tuned awareness? No doubt it is somewhat present in many a nascent social psychologist and is what drives him or her to formally study these strange forces that others do not seem to notice.

But greater social awareness can also be a result of that formal study. Besides "book learning," many social psychologists have gone through training explicitly designed to make them aware of the social interaction around them. In particular, social psychology professors often use "laboratory exercises" to demonstrate their points. They have their students engage in some interaction—for example, role play a conflict, or come to a group decision—and then use that experience as a basis for discussing the theories and research related to that experience. A perfect example comes, once again, from Lewin.

Fritz Heider (1983) described attending one of Kurt Lewin's seminars at the University of Berlin in the mid-1920s on a day when the subject was embarrassment. Rather than simply talk about it in the abstract, the ebullient Lewin embarrassed some people. He asked a male and female student to volunteer for a little "experiment." Then, upon agreeing, they were asked to dance in front of the class for several minutes, without music, while the rest of the students sat and watched. Afterward Lewin asked the pair about what they felt, and then brought the entire group into the discussion. By the end of class that day, those two students must have had a vivid experience of embarrassment, as seen by watching themselves watch others watch themselves, in a musicless waltz in a hall of mirrors.

Getting Sensitive

To many people the *T-group* (T for training), encounter group, sensitivity training group, or personal growth group was a fad of the 1970s. But before and after its public popularity, it was a serious technique for vividly teaching the patterns and dynamics of social life through direct experience. The T-group was officially born in 1946. We can think of that date as the moment when social psychologists' social sensitivity acquired a formalized technique for its development.

It all began when the Connecticut State Inter-Racial Commission asked Kurt Lewin to teach community leaders some new ways to combat racial and religious prejudice, a favorite topic of Lewin's. He and his cohorts planned a two-week workshop for forty-one selected trainees, mostly educators or social workers, about half of whom were black or Jewish. Lewin simultaneously planned to teach certain social principles, have the trainees experience those principles firsthand, and make all of this a research study to identify further the most effective methods of changing people.

In his usual democratic way, Lewin and all his staff of fellow social psychologists were to treat everyone as peers: the group would make decisions, not the "leaders." Thus on the very first day the group worked on making decisions about the next two weeks, while some of the researchers sat back to observe the group dynamics. That night the participants had the evening free while the staff met to hear the observers discuss what they had seen. Three of the participants had nothing planned for the evening and asked Lewin if they could sit in on the staff meeting. Some of the staff predicted mayhem, but Lewin probably made his famous response when disagreeing, in his pleasant German accent: "Could be, but I sink ozzer."

As one of the staff said about the meeting, it was as if a "tremendous electric charge" went through the room when people first heard their social behavior discussed (Marrow, 1969, p. 212, quoting Bradford). The charge sparked into an open conflagration when one trainee heard an observer's description of her behavior that did not fit with her own experience. She interrupted the staff and an intense interchange ensued—with Lewin in the middle of it, enjoying himself immensely, and turning it into a learning experience for the staff as much as for the trainees.

During this meeting no one was allowed to wander off into past histories or intellectual rationalizations for their behaviors. The topic was the "here and now" of what had happened that day, and clear feedback was the goal. Lewin was cheerfully confident that once people heard how their behavior affected others, they would be able to see for themselves what to change, be motivated to make the change, and be able to give clearer feedback to others. It was the hall of mirrors effect again—seeing oneself as others see one, and seeing how one responds to that, and how people react to that response, and how one responds to that reaction, and so forth.

The three trainees gained so much from this feedback about their "here and now" behavior that they asked if they could come back again. By the next night the word had gotten around and all forty-one trainees showed up after dinner to hear the observers talk about how they had behaved, and inevitably to discuss those observations.

A few nights later, after one of these meetings, Ronald Lippitt described how some of the staff discussed it "at a hamburger joint" and concluded that these sessions were having a powerful effect on the trainees' ability to bridge the gap between good intentions and actual behavior (Lippitt, quoted in Back, 1972, p. 9). Trainees could receive feedback that made them more sensitive to their behavior, and criticism was brought "into the open in a healthy and constructive way" (Lippitt quoted in Marrow, 1969, p. 212).

All in all, by the end of the two weeks, the evening sessions seemed to have been the most significant part of the workshop. This impression held up during the year after the workshop. The researchers kept track of the participants' efforts to combat discrimination and found they were making excellent progress. When asked about how the workshop had helped them, the trainees reported that their new sensitivity to their own behavior was one of the richest sources of growth, thanks especially to the feedback they had received during those evening sessions.

As a result, the next summer saw the establishment of the National Training Laboratories (NTL) in Bethel, Maine, designed to implement the discoveries of the first workshop by helping train leaders for communities around the country. Needless to say, the feedback, or training, session became central to the program, earning the name of T-group.[1]

Sadly, Lewin died before the first NTL session. But thanks to his "I sink ozzer," a powerful tool for research and social and personal change was born. NTL became almost synonymous with social and organizational change through small groups. More important, its T-group format refused to stay home in Bethel, Maine. It spread throughout North America under many names, finally reaching the West Coast in time to become synonymous with "touchy-feely" nude marathons and the me-generation, a far cry indeed from the social-change goals of its birth.

However these groups were used, they were used. Carl Rogers

(1968) called T-groups "the most significant social invention of this century." They have shown up in industry, education, family life, self-help organizations, and all the helping professions. Whatever they are called, the same principles tend to surface: feedback, hashing out misunderstandings, sticking to the here and now, reporting how other people's behavior makes one feel rather than prescribing how they ought to change, and supporting one another's attempts to try out new behaviors. Group members enter the hall of mirrors and, it is hoped, come out sensitive to what works when, with which people. And as for the training of social psychologists, T-groups frequently still play a major role, as the laboratory portion of courses in "small group process" or "interpersonal communications."

The Study of Interpersonal Communication

With all these group meetings being observed, and with the emphasis on research as well as training, it became important to find some way to summarize and compare the goings-on during these hundreds and thousands of hours of group meetings. Thus a whole new interest arose in what came later to be called "interpersonal communication."

Robert Bales pioneered in this area, beginning as one of the research team at the first Bethel workshops. The procedure he later formalized (Bales, 1950) as *Interaction Process Analysis*, simply involved watching groups interact and, each time a person said something, noting who spoke to whom and the kind of thing said (for example, "asks for information," "gives suggestion," or "shows agreement"). In other words, every statement was categorized in various simple ways. He also collected information after the meeting on who liked whom (a technique developed much earlier by J.L. Moreno) and other questions, such as who the group thought of as the leader.

This approach yielded some interesting discoveries. For example, Bales, along with Philip Slater (Bales, 1958; Bales & Slater, 1955; Slater, 1955), used it to study discussion groups they had set up with the task of solving a fictional management problem and found, first off, that the person who speaks most is usually also the one who is most often spoken to. More interesting, this person is also likely to be the one who is seen by the other members as having "contributed the best ideas for solving the problem" and having done "the most to guide the discussion and keep it moving effectively." These same individuals are also most likely to be rated by the members, after four sessions, as clearly being "the leader."

However, this same person who ranked high on all these fine qualities was usually *not* the best liked individual. Often this "task specialist" type of leader was the second most liked. But the "best liked" member was called a "socioemotional specialist" by these researchers, because he (all the participants were men) did not do much directly about getting the task done, but did the most to maintain group morale and harmony.

Also of interest was the fact that the two specialists tended to interact most with each other and to like each other more than they liked the other members of the group. Thus what Bales and Slater found is that a group spontaneously tends to find from among its members two people to play the roles of task and socioemotional specialists. They form a strong, internally cohesive coalition in the center of the group, much like parents in the traditional nuclear family.

While some groups elevate such leaders more than others, and while personality may play a role in which individuals end up serving in these roles, the development of these roles happens in *all* groups. It is a result of group interaction. It cannot be reduced to the effect of its parts. Group structures are real and independent of members. And social psychologists know this from their own personal observations of groups, whether as members or researchers.

Of course not all groups are T-groups or specially constructed groups for laboratory experiments. In fact, the most important ones are the ongoing ones found in offices, classrooms, factories, and homes. Methods like Bales's can only dig so deep into "what's really going on" in a busy, buzzing, fighting, loving ongoing group. To sense more complex dynamics, a well-trained human brain, simply observing and thinking about what's going on, is still very useful. What is even more useful is if that socially sensitive, intuitive mind can then turn its vague insights into testable hypotheses that can be verified experimentally and thus made explicit enough for anyone to use in their group life. This ability to verbalize and scientifically verify the unverbalized in a group is what makes the socially aware social psychologist a useful scientist, and not just a good party guest.

One of the most important kinds of small groups in any society is the family. Until recently, however, the family was considered too sacrosanct to study from the inside. But as the divorce rate has skyrocketed to almost 50 percent of marriages, and the problem of child abuse has loomed larger, the study of what really goes on in families has become significant, and even urgent. One researcher, John Gottman, of the University of Illinois, has been unusually good at quantifying the intangible feelings that rip back and forth between husband and wife in good and bad marriages.

Gottman (1979) brings into his laboratory two types of couples to study: those who have sought marital counseling and also reported their marriages to be not so hot, and those who have not sought counseling and are happy with their marriages. After years of preliminary observations, Gottman has arrived at several interesting techniques. For example, he has couples discuss the perennial six o'clock question of "How was your day today, dear?" And some of his analysis of the responses is done by the couples themselves. They sit at a table where they can push a lever backward or forward according to whether they are feeling good or bad as a result of what the other has said.

With this simple device, Gottman has verified some ideas which married couples can readily use. One is that the more negative the feelings produced by communications, the more likely it was an unhappy relationship! Another is that happily married spouses are as likely to respond to a negative statement with a positive one as with a negative response; they don't escalate their negativities the way unhappy couples do. Overall, happy couples are less predictable in their responses. They don't have standard scripts that they rely on for getting by or that they turn to during conflicts. (This makes them harder to study, but probably also makes them more interesting spouses.)

Finally, as any "socially sensitive" social psychologist and his or her spouse can testify, the fact that someone knows the "right thing to say" is no guarantee it will always be said. Gottman has found that spouses can watch another couple interact and know what to say to make the communication effective. But they do not necessarily use that skill with their own spouses (and those who do not are more likely to be in an unhappy marriage).

The study of nonverbal communication is another line of very practical "communications research" with roots in social psychologists' awareness of their social environment, and often with roots in their T-group experiences as well. If you are ever in a T-group, one of the things you will probably become intensely aware of is how much information about other people comes to you through their facial expressions, eye movements, posture, and tone of voice. But you don't need to be in a T-group to see this if you watch for it. Look around the next public place you enter—a classroom, a library, a store—and see how much you can tell about a person's recent life history, personality, and mood from nonverbal cues.

We all respond, often unconsciously, to many nonverbal messages. But our social successes escalate dramatically when we become alert to these nuances of expression. Suppose you are listening to someone give a talk. He sounds composed and assertive. But he's making some points you disagree with, so you eagerly plan your response.

Now imagine that you take your mind off your own response long enough to watch him more closely. A trembling hand gives him away—this speaker is nervous. You notice a twitch at the corner of his mouth too. Having made these additional observations, when you give your response you will probably begin by being supportive and reassuring (let's hope you don't use this knowledge to devastate the speaker). Quite possibly you will turn a potential adversary into an appreciative friend.

One often quoted study (Mehrabian & Ferris, 1967) found that of all the information conveyed to another person when we say something that is emotional (not informational), only 7 percent is contained in the actual meaning of the words we use. We can also thank nonverbal cues for the fact that we can all get along as well as we do with people who do not speak our language. The nonverbal "language" does vary from culture to culture, however. Consequently it sometimes creates greater misunderstandings than verbal ignorance, usually because people don't realize that there are differences across cultures in the meaning of certain gestures or facial expressions or of how far away one stands from the other when talking.

In our own culture, Marianne LaFrance and Clara Mayo (1976), social psychologists at Boston University, did a study comparing whites and blacks on the significance of looking the other person in the eye in conversations. They filmed a conversation of a black graduate student with a white executive, and another conversation of the same graduate student with a black institutional administrator, and laboriously analyzed the film, frame by frame, for who looked at whom and when. They also had teams of hidden observers watching two-person conversations at college cafeterias, fast food restaurants, and hospital and airport waiting rooms.

The observers rigorously timed the amount of time each person looked in the other person's eyes when listening. They found that whites tend to look at others when listening but not when talking; blacks tend to look at others when talking but not when listening. Thus whites and blacks easily misinterpret the messages they get when trying to know who should speak when. "When the white listener . . . encountered a pause with sustained gaze from a black speaker, the white was cued to speak, and both found themselves talking at once. . . . By directing his gaze at the black listener, the white speaker often did not succeed in yielding the floor and had to resort to direct verbal questioning" (p. 551). They note that such "miscues" and the necessity they may create for such things as direct questions, "may lend an unintentionally confrontational tone to the encounter" (p. 551).

Sometimes even when intercultural differences are not an issue, people often get into trouble by ignoring the nonverbal message, or think they have gotten it when they haven't. For example, people give certain nonverbal cues that show when they are lying; for example, they tend to speak in a higher tone of voice (Zuckerman, DePaulo, & Rosenthal, 1981). Most people are not aware enough of these cues, however, to use them either to lie well or to detect lying. Instead they tend to focus on facial expression, which is easily controlled by the liar. Gerald Miller and Judee Burgoon (1982), in an article intended to help lawyers assess "witness credibility," reviewed all of the social psychological research literature on lying. They concluded from several different studies that while people are quite convinced they can tell when someone is lying, in most of the studies they do no better than chance.

In short, much of the research done by social psychologists is an effort to translate their social awareness into testable hypotheses that will yield results that others can use. Or, sometimes social psychologists do their research just because they are curious about the underlying causes of the social phenomena they have observed. Either way, it is this intuitive sensitivity to these phenomena that is the prime source of much of their formal research. Let's see some other examples.

Honky Tonks and Hospital Beds Are All Grist for the Mill

Don Dutton is a well-known Canadian social psychologist who has conducted a series of studies of what he calls "reverse discrimination." According to this idea, during certain "trivial interactions," many middle-class whites treat minority group members better than they would other whites in the same circumstances. The inspiration for Dutton's research arose from an observation at the Park Plaza Hotel Bar, not far from the University of Toronto, in the early 1970s. The hotel had a policy and even a sign that it would not serve women in pants. But when a very well-groomed black woman came in wearing a pantsuit, the bartender, no doubt after some hesitation, served her as if nothing was amiss.

Recognizing this as an expression of a common but unresearched phenomenon, Dutton set to work studying the exact conditions in which reverse discrimination will arise. In his first such study (Dutton, 1971), he sent white couples and black couples in which the man was wearing a turtleneck, to fancy Vancouver and Toronto restaurants which did not allow tieless men. Of the twenty black couples that showed up, fifteen were allowed in. Of the twenty white couples, only six were allowed in. If the other race couple subsequently showed up, however, they were likely to get about the same treatment as the first couple, presumably because the restauranteur had to look consistent.[2]

Philip Zimbardo is a psychologist you will hear more of in subsequent chapters. Some of his most interesting research is on *deindividuation*, the way people can be stripped of their identities in certain "total" social environments, such as prisons, concentration camps, and armed forces boot camps. The way he first became interested in deindividuation is another good example of a social psychologist's sensitivity to social influences leading to a major line of research.

Zimbardo was in a serious automobile accident. He awoke to find himself in the trauma ward of a charity hospital that "looked like an old movie set for a prison camp film. It was physically deteriorated and filled with society's victims. . . . mostly alcoholics and derelicts who had been mugged for their last quarter" (1985, p. 567). All were "uniformed alike in their grubby green institutional pajamas" (p. 567), all except Zimbardo, who was still wearing his own shirt.

He kept wearing that red shirt, day after day. It became a sort of symbol of his difference, and the patients ignored him as long as he wore it. They made jokes about the shirt and him that clearly indicated that he was an outcast because he did not want to be dressed like them, much less be one of them. As a result, his sense of isolation grew.

Finally, one day Zimbardo took off the symbolic red shirt and donned the green pajamas. He was immediately accepted into the group. "The trauma ward was no longer traumatic for me—not home, but not so bad as it might look to an 'outsider' " (p. 567). He was part of the group's world at last.

Out of the hospital, Zimbardo became fascinated with the way he had lost his sense of individual identity and taken on the identity of the surrounding social group. He compared his experience to descriptions of people in concentration camps. Eventually he did a number of studies on this phenomenon, one of which is described in chapter 6.

Another, earlier study (Zimbardo, 1969) looked at whether people who were "deindividuated"—that is, made anonymous—would have fewer inhibitions about being aggressive. In this study, the subjects were groups of four female New York University college students who arrived at the experiment individually, and were dressed up by the experimenter in particular ways before they saw one another. In one condition their names were never used and they were dressed in oversize (size 44) lab coats and fitted with shapeless white hoods. (Judging from Zimbardo's photographs, the hoods were pillow cases with holes cut out for eyes and mouth. Although many discussions of this study liken the subjects' attire to KKK riders, to us they look more like Halloween trick-or-treaters.) In the other condition they were greeted by name, given a large name tag to wear, and were told that their unique reactions would be important.

The rest of the experiment was the same for both groups and rather complicated. In essence, all subjects had the opportunity to give someone shocks of various durations. The results? The anonymous, deindividuated students gave shocks that lasted twice as long as those given by the students with the large name tags.

So far we have described social psychologists as having chutzpah; a determination to demonstrate the reality of both social influence and its source, social groups; and a heightened subjective awareness of this social reality. In the next chapter you will see how all these characteristics set social psychology, in its early years, on a collision course with the rest of psychology. What happened when a self-righteous, authoritarian, well-entrenched status quo collided with a cocky, democratic rebellion? You are about to find out.

Notes

1. They were originally called *basic skills training groups*, or BST groups, but there were too many wisecracks.
2. Alas, Dutton's assistants did not get dinners at the restaurants, even if they were admitted. After being seated, they ordered drinks while supposedly waiting for the rest of their party to arrive, and then got a prearranged phone call, requiring them to leave. The calls got them out of there before research funds had to be spent on their suppers!

5

"Emperor's New Clothes Are Highlight of Royal Festivities"

I N the period in which social psychology grew up as a science, the 1930s through the 1950s, the dominant perspective in American psychology was *behaviorism*. You have probably heard before of this view that, if psychology is going to be scientific, psychologists must limit their data to the quantification of behavior, in particular the probabilities of seeing certain responses given that certain stimuli are present. Stimuli and responses, situations and behaviors—these can be reliably observed by anyone at any time. Thoughts, feelings, motivations—these can only be observed by the person having them. According to behaviorists, it is impossible to know if, for example, when I say I feel happy, I am referring to the same internal state as you experience when you say it. Behaviorists are famous for their opinion that the mind should be treated as a "black box." What goes in and goes out is a valid topic for science, but what goes on inside the walls of that magical box is beyond our ken.

Behaviorism swept psychology, beginning in 1913 with John Watson's "Psychology as the Behaviorist Views It." It is hard to fathom now the intensity of this movement. It was a reaction to "experimental introspection," a methodology that seemed hopelessly flawed, yet it was the main approach of psychology when Watson was a graduate student, around 1900. At that time psychology was defined as the study of human consciousness. But the new generation was having its doubts.

Geiwitz and Moursund (1979) claim that Watson "was uncomfortable using human subjects; he was shy, embarrassed, and awk-
ward. He was more comfortable with animals" (p. 94). So he taught
a rat to run a maze and wrote a paper, in the style of the day, trying
to interpret his observations in terms of the rat's consciousness, ending his sentences frequently with "if the rat has consciousness at all."

Not surprisingly, he got sick of the whole approach and in 1913
changed psychology forever with these opening four sentences of his
paper:

> Psychology as the behaviorist views it is a purely objective experi-
> mental branch of natural science. Its theoretical goal is the prediction
> and control of behavior. Introspection forms no essential part of its
> methods, nor is the scientific value of its data dependent upon the
> readiness with which they lend themselves to interpretation in terms
> of consciousness. The behaviorist, in his efforts to get a unitary scheme
> of animal response, recognizes no dividing line between man and
> brute. (p. 158)

Almost every specialization within psychology accepted Watson's
argument, bowing down under the relentless criticism of the young,
radical followers of Watson.[1] Every specialty capitulated except social
psychology. Social psychologists, almost without exception, continued to focus on the inner experience of people. They usually were
not shy and they certainly did not prefer to work with animals.

Thanks to this "heroic legacy," a haven was maintained within
psychology for those who wanted to research internal processes. In
particular, one important distinction was preserved and elaborated
on: there is a difference between what happens to people (the behaviorist's "stimuli") and how people *experience* what happens to them.
And if you want to understand what people will do (the behaviorist's
"response"), the crucial thing to understand in any research is not
what the experimenter observed, but what the subject observed. This
is called a *phenomenological* emphasis, and it was vehemently opposed
by behaviorism.[2]

The importance of this distinction between external events and
the internal experience of them has been accepted as almost an article
of faith by social psychologists, even during the dark years of behaviorism. When we brought up this question to various social psychologists, most of them huffily replied that "of course" social
psychology had always been cognitive. And people-based, not rat-

based. But then several admitted that it had been hard to be the only dissenters. As Jerry Singer said, "We took a beating" for it. Several even used the same phrase: "We were carrying the torch." And John Arrowood spoke of the "loneliness" of being the only faculty member on the hall holding such an outrageous position.

The position was held nonetheless. Then, around 1970, it became less lonely, as psychology finally threw off its behavioristic shackles and became largely "cognitive"—an emancipation which many social psychologists believe was due in part to their own courageous rebelliousness.

Why They Held Their Ground

We have to admit that not absolutely all social psychologists eschewed behaviorism. If you read chapter 3 you can guess the exception—Floyd Allport.[3] Allport was part of a long-standing American emphasis on the observable world and practical affairs, not vague thoughts and theories.

But his was not the general viewpoint. The general position was provided, once again, by Kurt Lewin. He had been part of the Gestalt revolution in Germany, which emphasized holistic perceptual and mental processes, in opposition to the "elementalism" and associationism of most of psychology. Associationism began in England and later took root in the United States, helping to shape behaviorism. It analyzed mental processes into discrete units, like mental atoms, and described a mental chemistry for how they combined.

Gestalt psychology, by claiming that mental processes such as perception, learning, and memory involved irreducible wholes instead of the accretion of tiny parts, had been a "loyal opposition" within European psychology for several decades. In Europe, academics had fought for their view on this issue with tremendous vehemence. Students of some professors holding one view could not even be seen in the company of professors from the other camp. So Kurt Lewin was used to this sort of furor. When he got to the United States and found behaviorism taking over, he was not about to give up studying the mind, or social perception, or social groups—or to stop thinking of these as wholes—just because some funny guy from North Carolina with a fondness for rats said it was not to his taste.

Lewin not only thought it was important to know how people

perceive and think; he really saw the observable world of stimuli and behaviors to be of only secondary importance. His reality was the "life space" of all the forces, ideas, memories, desires, and so forth that influenced the person at each moment in time. This was a mental world. Anything physical, or even social, was foreign to the life space. Unless the individual was *aware of* some "objective fact," it had no impact on the life space. Even the past did not matter, except as it was represented by current memories.[4]

Lewin's vision of the life space was his trademark even more than his *Quasselstrippe*, which we described in previous chapters. During every lecture he drew the oval life space diagram on the blackboard, or on a napkin, or in the dust, wherever was handy. Fritz Heider recalls that the first time Lewin spoke to him about the life space was on a cold winter evening in Berlin when they were waiting for a tram.

> He used the tip of his umbrella to trace a small circle enclosed by a larger oval on the snow-covered pavement. He explained that these figures represented the person within his own life space. Then he drew a little plus sign within the oval—that was the person's goal— and a line separating the person from the goal, which was the barrier. Thus he was able to represent many situations by means of [these diagrams]. (1983, p. 79)

One psychologist recalls that when Lewin would have the *Quasselstrippe* meetings at home, the floor would be covered with sheets of brown wrapping paper which they would use for diagramming the life space. "The 'full-fledged topologists' came to these sessions equipped with four-color pencils, to squat on their hands and knees and draw on wrapping paper" (Marrow, 1969, p. 89).

Lewin's students irreverently called these ovals "little eggs." And Lewin's students' students called them "bathtubs." But until well after Lewin's death in 1947, they were a trademark almost as much of social psychology as of Lewin. And although life space diagrams are no longer in fashion, the basic view of the mind as the essential reality continues to flourish and to spread, in spite of the temporary wet blanket tossed on by behaviorism. In social psychology, study after study has and will probably continue to distinguish between the situation as it is and the situation as the individual perceives it. It is as though every social psychologist has, watching over his or her shoulder, not Watson but Lewin, who made his point eloquently and for all time when he said,

> To describe a situation "objectively" in psychology actually means to describe the situation as a totality of those facts and only those facts which make up the field of that individual. To substitute for that world of the individual the world of the teacher, of the physicist, or of anybody else is to be, not objective, but wrong. (1942, p. 62)

It would be inaccurate to overemphasize Lewin's contribution on this point, however. Other pioneering social psychologists were just as adamant. Ted Newcomb said, "It seems to me to be a truism that no interpersonal behavior can be understood without a knowledge of how the relationship is perceived by the persons involved" (1947, p. 74). Solomon Asch—who, like Lewin, studied with the Gestaltists—said "it is not possible, as a rule, to conduct investigations in social psychology without including a reference to the experience of persons" (1959, p. 374). And the Sherifs, also Gestalt influenced, emphasized that "what an individual *does* . . . is not independent of the way in which he perceives the situation, appraises it, what he remembers at the time, and so on" (1969, p. 35).

Still, the deeper question remains: when the rest of psychology became so vehemently opposed to the study of the thinking process, why did Lewin, Newcomb, Asch, the Sherifs, and the rest of social psychology insist on this heresy? Much of it seemed to have to do with the strong interest in the formation and measurement of attitudes. The bulk of social psychology in the 1930s focused on attitudes, a very mental kind of thing. Why were attitudes important to early social psychologists? Zajonc (1980) thinks that it was part of their reaction to the rise of Naziism:

> American social psychologists asked themselves how it was possible for a nation like Germany, with one of the richest [cultural] . . . traditions, to change so rapidly . . . to tolerate the obliteration of . . . humanitarian . . . values. Germany was viewed as the product of a massive attitude change—a massive *cognitive* change—which was achieved by means of extremely effective propaganda.
>
> If political, economic, and social changes of unequaled scope can take place by virtue of persuasion . . . the role of cognitive processes in social life must be exceedingly important. How then could a social psychologist be anything but cognitive? (p. 189)

Lewin's most famous student, Leon Festinger, whom you will meet in the next chapter, explained it very simply: "From the point of view of understanding humans, if you look at nothing but behavior, you're ignoring a vast world that exists for human beings. . . . [If] you're concerned with creating a change in behavior that lasts and endures . . . something has to have gone on inside the person" (Festinger quoted in Evans, 1980, pp. 132–33).

And there may be one other reason. We have already discussed it: chutzpah. Social psychologists seem to enjoy shaking up the status quo. It was hard being cognitive in an era of entrenched, self-satisfied behaviorism. But it was also fun, and revolutionary. Perhaps for the radicals who began social psychology, it would have been harder to go along with the stuffy experimentalists down the hall than to fight them. In that sense they followed exactly in Watson's boots.

Impression Formation and Attribution Theory

For whatever reason, social psychology has been and is emphatically cognitive. Its methods and conclusions are usually the result of making a clear distinction between external and internal realities.

For example, there is only a small relationship between the similarity of two people's responses on an attitude questionnaire and their attraction to each other. But the relationship between these variables becomes strong when we see to it that they *perceive* a similarity, whether it is actual or not (Byrne, 1971).

In the area of stress on the job, the same amount of noise has fewer stressful effects if workers *believe* they have control over it (Glass and Singer, 1972). Or in the case of helping behavior, how likely people are to come to the aid of an injured person mainly depends on whether they perceive the person to be injured, whether they consider it to be their responsibility to help, and whether they think of themselves as capable of helping (Latane & Darley, 1970).

In almost every area of social psychology, the distinction between actual and perceived has been central. In fact, several areas are focused exactly on that. These are known by such names as "social perception" and "social cognition" and include what is currently the dominant theoretical perspective in the field, *attribution theory*. However, let's stay historical: first let us consider the grandparent of attribution theory, the study of *impression formation*, now an old timer as topics go, but still going strong.

Impression Formation—The Two Hannahs

Solomon Asch (1946), with his strong Gestalt background and interest in perceptual processes, started what became the study of impression formation. Right after World War II he did a study which found that if you ask people to form an impression of another person based on a list of descriptive terms, such as "warm, polite, honest, and busy," people do not give these terms equal weight as they form their impression. Certain terms, such as "warm" or "cold," contribute more to the impression than such "peripheral" terms as "polite" or "honest." On the battlefield against behaviorism, this was evidence that people do not passively respond to external stimuli. They reorganize information, putting some ahead of others. (And this goes on inside a *mind*, not a black box.)

Next let us introduce you to Harold Kelley, who took Asch's ideas further. Kelley became interested in social psychology while he was an undergraduate at Berkeley. During World War II he worked with the social psychologist Stuart Cook on a study of personnel selection for the armed forces. After the war, Cook went to New York to work on a project of Lewin's, and in the process, Kelley got to know Lewin and became his student. Many consider Kelley the greatest social psychologist still working today. He is certainly considered one of the nicest. While Jerry Singer was a graduate student at Minnesota, Kelley was on the faculty. Singer remembers,

> Hal was an incredibly good human being who cared about graduate students. He used to run sessions at his house over a series of weekends where he'd invite small groups of graduate students, his and everybody else's, just to spend an evening so that they'd get to know each other and have a cohesive group. He really cared about people. I have a lot of respect both for his intelligence and the stuff he's doing, and for him as a human being.

Similarly, John Arrowood, one of Kelley's former students, said, "He was a gentleman . . . we all knew that if there was anything that was bothering us, having to do with our academic or other research work, his door was always open."

One of Kelley's first studies (1950) examined how Asch's *central trait* idea affected impressions of actual people. Kelley told students in three classes at MIT that their professor could not come for the day, but that a guest lecturer would take his place and that he, Kelley, would like the students to evaluate the lecturer's performance afterward. The students received a note telling them a little about the instructor they would have, about his teaching experience, academic background, age, marital status, and such. For half the students, the note ended this way: "People who know him consider him to be a rather cold person, industrious, critical, practical, and determined." The other half received notes identical except that the words "very warm" were substituted for "rather cold."

The results were clear. During the class session 56 percent of the subjects with the "warm" description participated in the discussion, while only 32 percent of the "cold" description subjects did so. And on ratings of the instructor completed after class, the "warm" instructor was consistently rated more positively.

In his introduction to the study, Kelley wrote that it was based on Asch's work, in which "it proved to be necessary to postulate inner-observer variables which contribute to the impression and which remain relatively constant through time." Take that, John Watson.

Kelley's work was followed by many other studies on impression formation. Soon the topic's social relevance had expanded it into the study of stereotypes. Social psychologists wanted to know how distorted impressions were formed of, for example, racial or ethnic groups, men and women, or older people. This interest continues to the present. One fascinating, sophisticated example is a recent study by John Darley and Paget Gross (1983).

You may remember Darley as one of the researchers with Bibb Latane in the study of bystander intervention described in chapter 1. Darley was strongly influenced later by Solomon Asch, among others. But the interesting thing about Darley was that he knew Asch, Festinger, Kelley, and Schachter and all the other "greats" as a child. His father was chairman of the psychology department at the University of Minnesota during the era when anyone who was anyone at all in social psychology was, just had been, or soon would be a student or on the faculty. Darley reports, "I remember listening to their discussion in our living room. . . . Much of what I do . . . comes directly from those teachers" (quoted in Evans, 1980, p. 215).

Darley is a professor of psychology at Princeton, where, with Paget Gross, then a student, he looked more deeply at how stereotypes affect the information we use in making decisions about people. To put it in the enemy's terms, they examined how stimuli go into the black box and different behaviors come out, *depending on* the intervening thought processes.[5]

College students were shown one of two video tapes of a pretty, blonde, fourth grader named Hannah.[6] Students were randomly assigned to see one or the other of the tapes. Both tapes began with a four-minute segment of scenes of Hannah at a playground and around her neighborhood and school. One tape showed Hannah in a "stark fenced-in school yard" and "in an urban setting of rundown two-family homes." Her school was "a three-story brick structure set close to the street, with an adjacent asphalt school yard" (p. 23). In the other tape, Hannah was "playing in a tree-lined park," lived in an upper-middle-class suburban neighborhood, and attended a modern, sprawling school with playing fields and "a shaded playground." The college students also got a "fact sheet" about Hannah, stating that she was in the fourth grade and other basic information. All of this was the same for all subjects, except that those who saw the poor Hannah were told her parents had had only a high school education, and now her father was a meat packer and her mother a seamstress. In the other condition, Hannah's parents were both college graduates, an attorney and a freelance writer.

On the basis of the tape, *half* of the college students in *each* tape-viewing condition were asked to make an evaluation of Hannah's grade-level ability in various school subjects.

Surprise! Seeing the tapes seemed to have no effect: students from both groups rated the girl at about the fourth grade level in all the different subjects. In fact, many of the students very rationally refused to make a rating at all, saying they did not have enough information.

But here is where the study gets interesting. Darley and Gross then showed the remaining half of the students in each group another twelve minutes of video tape. This time they saw Hannah completing a school achievement test on which they could see both the questions and her answers to them, about two-thirds of which were correct. All the college students saw exactly the same tape for this part of the experiment.

When *these* students were asked to rate Hannah's grade level on various subjects, suddenly their responses showed the effect of seeing one or the other of the two previous tapes. Those who had seen a poor Hannah said she showed low ability; those who had seen an affluent Hannah credited her with abilities that were a grade level higher.

What happened? From other questions about the ratings, Darley and Gross found that the viewers did form a hypothesis about Hannah based on their initial impression, but they were not willing to act on that hypothesis without more information. However, the subsequent objective information was not used objectively; it was used to confirm the hypothesis. Those subjects who thought Hannah was a child of the upper class saw the test she took as more difficult, remembered her as answering more items correctly, and recalled more positive behaviors, such as paying close attention to questions, and fewer negative ones, such as staring off into space. The opposite was true of those who thought she came from a lower-class background.

The study has many messages, both theoretical and practical. For this chapter's purposes, it is enough to point out again that this kind of research requires a focus on subjective experience. True, certain "stimuli" have certain "associations," but that is about all that can easily be said of this study from a behaviorist's point of view. Nor would a behaviorist probably have done such a study, given the impossibility of knowing the conditioning history of the subjects. The behaviorist might privately wish, "If we could raise humans in little cages, under identical conditions . . ." And the social psychologist would know the result would be a bunch of total social misfits. Humans cannot be separated from their social environment and the set of experiences each has gained from that environment. As a result, humans will never be good subjects for the studies behaviorists need to do to confirm their theories.

Attribution Theory: Part I
Flighty Fritz and His Film of Flitting Forms

The currently most influential theoretical perspective in social psychology, *attribution theory*, is an approach to understanding people that is fundamentally an analysis of how people *think* about their world. It says that people do not just passively observe, but spontaneously evaluate and attribute causes for what they see, especially if what they are seeing is another person (rather than nonsense syllables, as in a verbal learning experiment).

For example, if a friend forgets your birthday, do you simply observe the nonevent and let it go? No, if you are like most of us, you attribute the forgetting to the person not liking you, to the person being thoughtless, to the person being very busy right now, or to the possibility that there's going to be a surprise party any minute. We humans are such full-time attributors, especially of social events, that it is a wonder social psychology didn't begin with this topic.

Actually, it practically did. But the man who was first interested in attribution was such a laid-back fellow that it took him a few decades to write the seminal book. And it took a couple more decades for anyone to notice it, since Fritz Heider was not the charismatic sort. But in time his book became topic number 1 on everyone's list.

Fritz Heider was a close friend of Lewin's from the start, but they were very different types. Fritz grew up in Austria, the son of a well-to-do architect and amateur archeologist (for an account of his life, see Heider, 1983). And Fritz had a reputation for being a flighty dilettante.

He wasn't lazy; he just couldn't settle onto one project for life. He began studying architecture, then switched to law, then to philosophy and psychology. But this chronology only begins to capture the variety of his interests. His autobiography tells of an endless round of studying this and that, here and there, during an "extended adolescence." He took trips to Italy at whim, and to Berlin for a year or two. He had countless jobs, from installing burglar alarms to teaching at an orphanage. Lewin tried to help him with a job making lampshades; Fritz lasted for four shades. His parents were delighted and amazed when he earned his doctorate (he wrote that he did it mainly because everyone else was and it seemed easy). But his wanderlust was a saving characteristic when it made him say yes on a moment's notice to a suggestion that he go to the United States to work in a psychology laboratory at a school for the deaf (with the famous Gestalt psychologist Kurt Koffka). As a result, he was out of Germany when Hitler rose to power and in a position to help others, like Lewin, make their move when it became necessary.

In Northampton, Massachusetts, in the laboratory at the school for the deaf, Heider met Grace Moore. With his typical lack of hesitation, three months later they had decided to marry. Grace proved to be the necessary ballast; the two stayed married. And they have only moved once since, from Northampton, where Heider eventually taught at Smith College, to the University of Kansas, at Lawrence.

Lewin, in contrast, was the son of a middle-class shopkeeper. The Lewins were Jews in East Prussia, so Kurt knew all about prejudice and hard times. He worked very hard at his education and knew exactly what he wanted—an academic position, even though as a Jew he knew that a good position with tenure was impossible. He stayed put in Berlin, and it was very difficult for him emotionally to emigrate when it became necessary. Lewin was relentlessly extroverted and social; Fritz Heider was more of an introvert. Lewin was also something of a type A personality, with hundreds of projects going on at once; it took Fritz years to produce his few books. As a result perhaps, Lewin died of a heart attack when he was fifty-seven, and Fritz finished his autobiography in 1983 at the age of eighty-seven.

The tortoise takes his time, but his accomplishments may become legendary. This is especially true in the case of Heider. He was an observer at the periphery for a long time, taking up Lewin's ideas, those of Henry Murray, a personality psychologist, and even those of Clark Hull, a learning psychologist. But he abandoned these ideas when they didn't help him understand his particular interest, interpersonal relations. Harold Kelley says his own impression of Heider was like everyone's—"he was a dreamy, thoughtful, converted-artist, aesthetic kind of person—doing these very off-the-wall, out-of-the-field things. Then they'd turn out finally to be exceedingly important."

The birth of attribution theory is the best example of what Kelley is talking about. It seems that Heider wanted to understand how people's commonsense observations of others affect their relationships. With his student Marianne Simmel (see Heider & Simmel, 1944), he made a film of geometric forms and showed them to people. (He had used the same forms at the school for the deaf to study puzzle-solving.)

Unlikely as the approach sounds, it led to something. He found that everyone watching films of these shapes moving around would, quite spontaneously, describe the action in terms of people: the tri-angles were men, the circles were women, they fought, loved, had happy reunions, got in and out of balance with each other. The universality of these perceptions was quite astounding.

These *attributions* were the beginning of attribution theory. If people attributed so much to mere objects, Heider reasoned that they must attribute much more to people. From that insight he developed his now famous ideas.

Attribution Theory: Part II
Of Nudes and Quiz Shows

Heider began to write about attribution around 1944, but the theory did not meander into the mainstream of social psychology until the mid-1960s, when it was revived simultaneously by several research-ers. Of these, Hal Kelley's contribution was the most influential.

Kelley told us that at the University of Minnesota the faculty held regular meetings where they would report on various books they had agreed to read for the group's information. Kelley acquiesced to reading Heider's (1958) book, a work that he says he certainly would never have looked at with much care had he not been obliged to. However, he liked the book so much that he wrote a paper on attribution for the Nebraska Symposium on Motivation (Kelley, 1967). In it he took Heider's fairly general notions and put them in terms that were not only easy to test experimentally but also related to social psychologists' own experience as researchers. The paper has been very influential.

From that time to the present, attribution theory has become the most important theoretical topic in the field. In the mid-1960s, when Kelley first discussed the theory, the major social psychology jour-nals had virtually no research on this topic. Ten years later, one in every twelve articles was explicitly concerned with attribution theory (Lamberth, 1980) and a great many of the others made reference to it in their discussion of results.

Again, what is central to attribution theory is the distinction it makes between what is actual and what people perceive to be the case. This distinction is important in understanding both people's attributions about others and about themselves. For example, with regard to attributions people make about themselves, Stuart Valins

(1966) asked male college students to look at slides in order to judge the attractiveness of ten different nude women depicted in the slides. As they were seeing the pictures, one at a time, they were also listening through earphones to what they thought was their heart rate. When the experimenters made the "heart rate" increase during a particular slide, that slide was rated as more attractive. Also, when the subjects were given the opportunity to take some of the slides home with them, these were the slides they selected. Thus, in this study, the subjects attributed their (supposed) increased heart rates to their attraction to the slide. (More precisely, Valins suggests that when they heard their own heart beat increase, they looked closely at the slide to "confirm" their hypothesis that the picture was in fact more arousing.)

Given that people's subjective attributions of the cause of an event are more important than what objectively caused it, the next issue is what determines these attributions. This question is mainly asked regarding how people explain the causes of others' behavior; one of the most important answers came from Lee Ross.

Ross, originally a student of Stanley Schachter's and now a professor of social psychology at Stanford, first gave a name to a "phenomenon long familiar to social psychologists in the Lewinian tradition"—the *fundamental attribution error*. This is the tendency of people to explain other people's actions as due to personality characteristics rather than the situation, no matter how inappropriate. For example, if someone lies, we tend to say that person is dishonest, whatever the social pressure he or she was under.

Ross became aware of the fundamental attribution error, he told us, at the oral examinations of two doctoral candidates. At the first, his own examination, he recalls that he felt in great awe of the important scholars who were examining him. They seemed to have so much more knowledge and ability than he. But one year later he was a professor examining a doctoral student, and although he had not learned that much in one year, he realized that the student saw him as an important scholar with much more knowledge and ability. The professors saw one another that way too. Everybody was making the attribution error—seeing others in terms of personal characteristics, when the only important difference was their relative social positions, which had been emphasized by their roles at the examination.

Thus Lee Ross and two of his students, Teresa Amabile and Julia Steinmetz, conducted what has become a famous attribution study (1977). Pairs of college students who did not know each other participated in the experiment. When they arrived, one of each pair was arbitrarily designated "questioner" and one "contestant" in a "quiz show game." The questioners were asked to make up ten fairly difficult questions to which they happened to know the answers, and then to ask them. On the average, the contestants could answer about six.

At the end of the experiment each participant was asked to rate the other's "general knowledge"—not the specific knowledge the questions were on. In almost every case the contestants thought the questioners were more *generally* knowledgeable than themselves. Even uninvolved observers tended to make the same judgments. While everyone was aware that the questioner had the advantage in asking questions to which he knew the answers, the difference was perceived as due to personal characteristics.

This distinction is not just some abstract principle. Think about how much difference it makes, for example, if a husband is upset by something his wife has done and, although in fact the action was necessitated by circumstances, he sees it as another instance of her fundamental "carelessness" or "lack of consideration." One social psychologist, in fact, explained that he first became aware of the operation of the fundamental attribution error in his life when he noticed that even though his wife was at least as knowledgeable and intelligent as his eminent male colleagues, they saw her as less so, probably because women are taught not to exert control over what is talked about in a discussion. But this difference was perceived by his male colleagues as a personal characteristic—that she knew less!

The Ultimate Study of the Importance of Subjective Reality

Social psychology of just about every kind depends on this assumption that subjective reality is important. That is, that since "what is real is what has an effect," the subjective must be real, given its important intervening role between situation and response. Perhaps the most striking evidence of the power of the subjective comes from a study by Abraham Tesser of the University of Georgia.

Abe Tesser is a slight, bright-eyed, enthusiastic lover of new ideas and clever research. Abe is such a firm believer in the reality and influence of mental processes that he wondered if the process of polarization in groups (see chapter 3) may happen in people's minds as well, without any group to discuss the issue with. That is, if you have an opinion about something and then have a chance merely to think more about it, instead of becoming more moderate in your opinion, could your original viewpoint shift to a more extreme position? Could this happen just by thinking about an issue, on your own?

To see, Tesser did a very simple experiment. On each of several issues, subjects were first asked to indicate how much they agreed or disagreed with a statement such as, "In many cases, revolution is the best way to correct political and social problems" (Tesser, 1978, p. 299). Then they were given a few seconds to think about the statement and asked to rate their agreement or disagreement again. Of those given thirty seconds to think, about 25 percent gave more emphatic ratings than their original feeling. Of those given two minutes to think, 65 percent became more emphatic.

Tesser and his students and colleagues have conducted a series of such studies on a range of topics, from opinions on social issues to impressions of people. In each case, as Tesser concludes, "simply thinking about some object can result in attitude change" (p. 304). This all comes about, he explains, because when we think about something, other associated mental structures get connected up and add to the original thought's significance. The mental world is a powerful kingdom.

Tesser said of his work,

> Underlying much of the idea of self-generated attitude change is the notion that the world is really a construction and these [mental structures] help us to construct it. Without the [mental structures], there is no construction. If there's no construction, there's no change.

The main scientific journal in social psychology today is the *Journal of Personality and Social Psychology*, known in the field as JPSP. In the last few years, each issue has been divided into three parts. One part is for the personality psychologists (who feel they are being taken over by social psychology, which may be true at least for now). The other two parts are labeled Interpersonal Relations and Group Processes, and Attitudes and Social Cognition. The latter topic, (which is actually part I of the journal) is typically the fattest.

Social cognition refers to the way the mind handles the social world. In many ways this perspective is not very different from the cognitive psychology which has taken over much of mainstream experimental psychology. But social psychology's version of cognitive psychology differs in being concerned with cognition in the real world, of *people*—both people's perception of others and how others affect what people perceive. Nor does this version ignore the feelings people have. Thus one social psychologist we spoke to characterized the "other" cognitive psychology (the non-social psychology) as "juiceless"—and started to say "useless" as well, before correcting herself!

That's okay. We should have expected that social psychology's study of cognition would be especially spirited.

In the next chapter you will finally see social psychologists at work (for them, play) doing their research. We'll let them tell you about it, step by step, then take you on a behind-the-scenes tour of one study. At least according to social psychologists, the next chapter's topic should be great fun.

Notes

1. Besides being shy, in his youth Watson is said by Schultz (1975) to have been "indolent, argumentative, and not easily controlled." He fought a great deal and was twice arrested, once for shooting firearms inside the city limits of his hometown. While attending the University of Chicago he found the famous John Dewey "incomprehensible." Later his career of turning psychology upside down was abruptly ended by his affair with a laboratory assistant, which led to a highly publicized divorce and his resignation from Johns Hopkins University. He went on to make a fortune in advertising, where he "did things in great style and loved to show a display of power" (Larson and Sullivan, p. 352, quoted in Schultz). All in all, he is an easy person to cast as a semi-villain!

2. On one point all of psychology did capitulate, and rightly so: that we can never know for sure what has gone on inside a mind, especially if it is not our own. We can only observe behavior and situations. But social psychologists generally believe there is no reason they can't use their observations to infer what went on mentally. In fact, not to try to make these inferences tends to make us poorer predictors of behavior, as well as students of the trivial.

3. A later exception is Daryl Bem. Like Floyd Allport, Bem describes himself as a bit of a loner. You'll learn more about this interesting character in chapter 7. Bem came to social psychology via physics and says he "never had a mentor" in the usual, traditional sense of social psychology—so he has an excuse.

4. Lewin first thought of the life space when he was a soldier during World War I. War was as traumatic for him as anyone, but he was fascinated by his own responses to it. He wrote an article on "The War Landscape" in which he described how a landscape is perceived as open and without direction in peace, but in war, as the soldier proceeds toward the front lines, he sees the landscape in terms of favorable positions for defending himself and places where food and shelter might be had, and as having a front and back, boundaries and zones. Objects in a battle zone become the soldier's property, not because he fought for them, but because the soldier sees everything as existing for military purposes. Prior to World War I, Lewin had actually done considerable research on associationism. But he gave it up around 1917, certain that a major modification in theory was needed, no doubt in part because of these experiences (Marrow, 1969).

5. At some point we must be fair to Watson, Skinner, and all the rest. *In theory*, behaviorism can probably explain anything without any reference to internal states, even if a cognitive approach seems more sensible. We merely need to know the entire conditioning history of each individual. If a person reacts to the word "warm" or makes jokes about some ethnic group, he or she has been reinforced for this behavior in the past, or these responses are associated with certain stimuli. Words can be stimuli. Reinforcers can be social. Or they can be "secondary," so that if we associate laughter with mother, and mother with food, then if someone laughs at our ethnic joke, we are being reinforced. Even our own thoughts can reinforce us in modern behavioral theories. But the whole construction got so complicated—and the behaviorists had ruled the roost for so long, with so little graciousness—that at some point it was easier to start over rather than continue to remodel the old coop.

6. Was this choice of a name a tribute to Kurt Lewin? Lewin's popularity in the United States began when he attended the 1929 meeting of the American Psychological Association. Although he spoke little English, his tremendous enthusiasm about social psychology impressed even those who could not understand his German. Also impressive, apparently, was a film he brought along of a toddler. The film demonstrated his principle of forces in a field, and the little girl's name was Hannah.

6

"Hey, You Guys on the Trapeze, Can I Ask You a Few Questions?"

JOHN Arrowood is a University of Toronto social psychologist who studies social comparison processes. He was a student of Harold Kelley and Stanley Schachter during the exciting period when they were both at the University of Minnesota. But to us, Arrowood's chief claim to fame will always be the playful pleasure he took in being my[1] dissertation advisor when, rather than showing an interest in his research, I took on what was by 1970 standards an outlandishly ridiculous dissertation project.

Arrowood is tall, lean,[2] bearded, charming, and a wonderful storyteller. His eyes sparkle when he gets into a good one. I could just see the gleam in his eye when I asked him on the telephone why he had entered the field. His reply:

> I had an undergraduate research scholarship for a summer and got to meet a number of . . . social psychologists who all seemed to be having the time of their lives doing things that you probably couldn't have stopped them from doing anyway. They were professionally nosy, they were curious. They were finding out new things—and they were getting *paid* for doing it!
>
> This came as a great revelation to me, because I had thought up to this point that the only people that ever got paid for doing something that you couldn't stop them from doing were hookers. And I've subsequently learned (through studying sociology) that hookers don't particularly enjoy it.
>
> The people that I met were really enjoying what they were doing.

And so I was hooked at that point on research. There was simply no thought thereafter of going into law school.

Ellen Berscheid, who is the 1984–85 recipient of the Donald Campbell Award for Distinguished Research in Social Psychology as well as the 1984 president of the Society for Personality and Social Psychology, tells another story of being seduced by research. She was majoring in literature at the University of Nevada when she took a psychology course. She did not enjoy the course, but she impressed her professor, Paul Secord, who asked her to help on a research project. She loved the work, and when she was told she would have to become a psychology major to continue it, she reluctantly did so.

Later she married and moved to Minnesota where she took a job with Pillsbury, doing research. She was promoted further than any previous woman, but the prejudice was still too much and she quit to take a job as a research assistant to Elliot Aronson (a consumate researcher whom you'll get to know later). Again she was told she could not do research unless she was a graduate student in psychology. So she signed on, took the courses "the other kids in the lab were taking," "took the exams they took," and "before I knew it I had my doctorate." All for the love of research.

Perhaps Jerry Singer sums up these feelings about research best:

> It's just a satisfying feeling . . . when I'm doing it, things feel right. . . . Getting the idea, going in and operationalizing it in the lab . . . piloting until it works, getting the study started and saying, "Hey it's off the ground, it's going!"

It is our impression that social psychologists enjoy most of their work—research, theorizing, writing, presenting papers, teaching, consulting, discussing their work with colleagues and the public, and all the rest. But their favorite part almost invariably is the actual research. In this chapter we are going to break that activity down into parts: reviewing the literature, planning the research, carrying it out, analyzing the data, and writing the study up. In each case we will let social psychologists describe how they feel about it. Then we will give you one example from start to finish of what goes on inside a social psychologist's head while doing research. The example is one we know very well, since I did the studies myself.

A Look at Each of the Parts

Getting the idea is the first stage. But that has to do with theory, another area of social psychological pleasure, which we will consider in detail in the next chapter. Once an idea is in the wings, the show begins.

Reviewing the Literature

It may sound tedious, reading everything related to the topic you want to research, but it is exciting too, as well as necessary.[3] You never know where your search will lead you, especially once you have become an expert in some specialized topic no one else knows as well as you. Morton Deutsch's first assignment as Lewin's graduate student was to review the literature on prejudice and intergroup relations. His next assignment was to use what he learned, by serving as a consultant to a Detroit school system.

One of our interviewees, Anthony Greenwald (a social psychologist at The Ohio State University), provides a good sense for the discoveries one can make within the literature:

> There are few things that are more satisfying than discovering that something you are now reading fills in a gap, or allows you to see how things can be combined in a way that you couldn't see before. The strongest example was when I discovered William James's treatment of idiomotor action, which helped produce a *Psychological Review* article on idiomotor theory. So I discovered something in that case that had been written in 1890.

Harold Kelley's entire career was changed by working with John Thibaut on a review of the literature on group problem solving and process for a chapter for the *Handbook of Social Psychology* (1964). He remembered the job as being fun: "Seeing frameworks, seeing order, seeing that the field does cumulate. It does build up brick by brick by brick. . . . I enjoy that." But "the most exciting part was two minds digging stuff out and clicking." The two men had known each other since their days as students of Kurt Lewin, but this was the first time they had recognized their potential as a team. As a result of this project, Kelley discovered a congenial collaborator in John Thibaut. They went on to write much more together, and to create their famous and fruitful *exchange theory* (1958, 1978). All in all, Kelley says this review of the literature "was the beginning of the most important intellectual development of my career."

In other words, when some social psychologist casually slips out the door saying, "I think I'll go on over to the library and review the literature a little while," you never know what is going to come of it.

Planning the Research

This next step may be the most exciting of all: going from the idea, in the light of a thorough knowledge of what's been done before in the area, to designing the actual procedures.

Elliot Aronson is a recognized master of the laboratory social psychology experiment. Lee Ross said that when planning an experiment, "I'd rather have ten minutes with Elliot than an hour with anyone else." And Aronson tends to talk about another famous researcher, Leon Festinger, when he describes the planning process:

> Festinger always said good ideas are a dime a dozen. The important thing is to take that idea and translate it into a set of experimental operations. . . . It's absolutely true. I see it as a very creative process. You get stimulated by an idea. Then the skill has to come. The real excitement is . . . constructing it so you can put it away for six months and go back to it and say "that's about the only way that could have been done."
>
> There's a wonderful scene in "Amadeus," when Mozart writes an opera and the emperor comes in and says "too many notes." Mozart says, "It couldn't have been done any differently." And I think that's the way I feel about certain experiments. They couldn't have been done any differently.
>
> . . . The casting of the scenario—I think that it must be the same kind of thrill that a novelist gets, or a playwright. And yet it's more interesting to me because it's in the interest of science, it's in the interest of truth.
>
> . . . You work it out and work it out and work it out, and what you come up with is a wonderful tapestry. And the critic comes along and says, "Ah but that little thread in the tapestry is wrong and if you only could have replaced it with this." And then you realize that if you pull that thread, the whole thing is going to unravel. You can't just change one thing. You have to say, "If you don't like that scenario, you try one."

Aronson likens the work of the researcher to that of a dramatist; a social psychology experiment is a special re-creation of ordinary life. At its best it reveals that life to us. Or as Lee Ross (known for his fundamental attribution error quiz-show experiment) put it, an experiment can be thought of as a demonstration: "It's not so much a way of testing an idea, but a way of communicating an idea. It's producing a metaphor, or maybe an anecdote, or a vignette that allows you to communicate a point."

We have seen this element of drama and teaching in many of the studies described in previous chapters—from Lewin's study of leadership in boys' groups to Sherif's Robber's Cave studies, from Milgram's obedience and Asch's conformity studies to Schachter and Singer's experiments on the cognitive determinants of emotion. But perhaps the ultimate demonstration was done by Philip Zimbardo.

Phil Zimbardo is one of social psychology's consumate showmen. (You will remember him from chapter 4 as the man with the red shirt.) During the early seventies he would often arrive to give scientific presentations wearing a long, flowing cape—which he would dramatically flourish at appropriate points during his presentation. Zimbardo can bring this off because he is well respected for the rigor and creativity of his research. But his cape-wearing is not unrelated to his style of research. When we asked him what he loves about planning research, he said:

> Just being aware of endless options at every point. . . . How you word things. How you present and how you arrange the laboratory. Each decision is challenging, and can mean that a good idea will seem to be shown not to work, just because you've decided wrong. . . . It's risk taking.

We asked about the relation of social psychology research to drama.

> What I do is straight theater. In fact, I co-teach a course now in psychology and drama. In many of my studies I have a script, a prepared scenario. There is scenery . . . there're actors. The only thing that's left to vary is the subject's response. That's the only improvisational part. Everything else is totally scripted. . . . And if you have it all down right and you have a good theory, then the audience applauds at the end exactly the way they're supposed to. And if your theory is not good, or the acting is not good, or the staging is not good, then it misses.

Now for our promised ultimate example of planning a dramatic study. Zimbardo, along with Craig Haney and W. Curtis Banks (Haney, Banks, Zimbardo, 1973), were interested in the topic of deindividuation, or the way that a dehumanizing environment can totally change people in predictable ways in spite of their individual personalities. They were also interested in prisons, and in the fact that deplorable prison conditions are not being changed, even though, in their present state prisons are known to be costly and ineffective. Zimbardo and his colleagues suspected this is at least in part because people believe prisons are inevitably bad places because bad people fill them. So these researchers set out to demonstrate that completely normal people, in a genuine prison environment, will quickly develop the same dehumanizing social environment seen in all prisons. In other words, when the scene on stage is a prison, this stage comes to control the actors, not the actors the stage.

Here comes the wonderful planning. To create "a genuine prison environment" that was still legal, safe for subjects, and under their control, the researchers walled off a part of the basement of the psychology building at Stanford University. Three 6- by 9-foot cells were made, with steel-barred doors and no furniture except cots. A 2- by 2- by 7-foot unlit closet served as a potential solitary confinement. There were also a "yard" for exercise and guards' quarters nearby.

Zimbardo, Haney, and Banks also decided to provide uniforms in order to increase anonymity: guards would wear khakis, a whistle, a police nightstick, and reflective sunglasses; the prisoners would wear loose-fitting muslin smocks, without underwear, and with an ID number on front and back, plus a chain and lock around one ankle, rubber sandals, and a nylon stocking cap. No personal belongings would be allowed.

They decided to recruit subjects with an advertisement asking for college students to be in a "study of prison life" and offering $15.00 a day for two weeks. Seventy-five applied. The "most normal" twenty-two were selected after extensive interviewing. These were randomly assigned to be guards or prisoners.

Guards were told they would serve eight-hour shifts. Their purpose was to maintain order, but they could not use physical force. Prisoners were to be given three supervised toilet visits and two hours of reading or letter writing a day, daily work assignments, two visiting periods per week, plus movie rights and exercise periods.

The students who would be prisoners were told to be available at their home or dormitory one Sunday night. Zimbardo arranged to have them "arrested" by the Palo Alto City Police. They were charged, advised of their legal rights, handcuffed, carried to the police station in the rear of a squad car, booked, fingerprinted, questioned enough to prepare an ID file, then placed in a detention cell. Next they were blindfolded and driven to the mock prison, where they were stripped, sprayed with a delousing solution, and made to stand alone, naked, in the cell yard, until given uniforms, photographed, and led to a cell. They were greeted and told the rules, to be memorized, and were thereafter told they would be referred to only by the numbers on their uniforms.

The researchers (now "wardens") had told the prisoners and guards that they were "free" to do whatever they wanted in their roles, as long as they followed the minimal "regulations." But in fact, as a result of all this careful planning of scene and set, this stage produced very decided role-taking. The guards became more and more abusive with their power as the prisoners became more and more passive. Privileges were never granted and mere eating, sleeping, and eliminating became rewards rather than rights, rewards that were frequently denied. The level of psychological cruelty was quite extreme; the guards harassed, threatened, and insulted the prisoners, who did little to defend themselves. One went on a hunger strike, but the other prisoners, at the guards' encouragement, turned on him rather than joining him. Guards were always on time for their shifts and frequently stayed after. When the study finally was stopped, after only six days, the guards were actually disappointed. But the prisoners were so delighted that all but one was willing to quit even without being paid. Actually, five already had "quit"—with extreme reactions of depression, crying, rage, anxiety, and physical symptoms that required removing them early from the simulation.

The postexperiment period required equal planning, especially once the experimenters saw the extent of the involvement of these quite normal students. All the participants met with the experimenters on several occasions over a year's time to talk about the experience, learn from it, and be certain there were no lasting effects.

(Zimbardo thinks they were, in the end, better off for the experience.) All the subjects, and also the experimenters, were surprised by how potent the simulation had been. While it probably was painful for Zimbardo, Banks, and Haney to see they had caused so much suffering and sadism in normal people, it certainly must have been exciting to see their careful planning result in such strong effects, and, more important, to demonstrate a point they hope will save a great deal of suffering in the long run.

Nearly everyone we spoke to about the process of planning an experiment emphasized how much of the pleasure was in planning it *with others*. The *Quasselstrippe* which followed Lewin around all his life is re-created in the planning of almost every social psychological experiment. As social psychologist Bill Graziano of the University of Georgia put it,

> It's a great deal of fun taking fairly abstract theoretical ideas and translating them into viable research. . . . Personally, I don't like doing that by myself, I like doing that with other people. It's a very stimulating social encounter to have other people to bounce ideas off. . . . Usually it's a fairly protracted kind of interaction. You may get a brilliant idea for a research project but you're never going to be able to put it into a researchable form in a brief encounter.

Carrying out the Research

This stage varies a lot, and that may be the best part of it. One may be conducting surveys, directing a scene, introducing strangers— anything at all. While researchers do not always do this stage themselves, for methodological reasons, they are always close by and eagerly involved. Anything can happen, and that is also part of the fun.

We asked Zimbardo about how he felt about actually carrying out research, or what is called "running subjects" in an experiment (the phrase may have slipped in from behaviorists, who run rats through mazes):

> It's all discovery. Discovering individual differences, idiosyncratic reactions, seeing the phenomenon work first hand. Because without it all you have is numbers. You may as well have a pigeon in a Skinner box pressing a lever and generating numbers. What you anticipated

with your formal . . . measures, that may not be all there is. If you don't actually run the subjects or observe them being run, you're not as likely to think about other questions to ask.

Analyzing the Data

If you are not fond of mathematics, statistics, and computers, this step can sound rather forbidding. But in fact, it is the most exciting part for many people, because it is the Moment of Truth. Did all that thinking, planning, and running of subjects produce something or not?

Graziano described this aspect very vividly:

I really enjoy looking at the outcomes. . . . It's great fun, just great fun. Just throwing the [data] around. Trying to carve nature at its joints and you don't know where the joints are. Now there's an experience. Actually, it's more like carving jello at its joints. At least with the data I get.

And Harold Kelley commented:

I really enjoy nothing more, hardly, than sitting down and analyzing a set of data that I don't fully understand and that I sense have some structure and information to be extracted if I'm clever enough to capture it.

Yet another social psychologist, Russ Fazio, emphasized the discovery process.

For me that's the most exciting part. I will sit there and play with data for a long time. . . . Use some rank-ordering techniques. Just try to get some feel for what's there. Trying to see things that kind of pop out that you might not have thought to look for otherwise. It allows for some creativity. What if I look at only this particular subsample, what would I find—things of that sort. It can be fun just to see where your ideas lead you.

And of course, there *is* that Moment of Truth. Fazio continued:

That can be very exciting or very frustrating. I've certainly walked away from the office at the end of the day feeling very good, just very high about everything because data have come in as I expected. Or walked away feeling incredibly puzzled. Even depressed. There is that moment of truth.

Just as there is a bit of theater in social psychologists, there is a bit of the gambler too. Winning is fun—all the more so since winning adds knowledge to the world.

Writing It Up

The final phase of research is letting people know about it, usually by writing a research article to be submitted to one of the journals in the field. It may be accepted as is. More likely, the editor recommends "publish with revisions." Then you receive the comments of two or three anonymous reviewers (who supposedly don't know your name either, except it is often possible for both sides to guess) and take their advice into consideration. Or you may receive a rejection, with reasons, usually suggesting further research you might undertake to strengthen the article for submission to a different journal.

You might also present your research at a convention, conference, or annual meeting of, for example, the American Psychological Association. There you might be scheduled to give your paper at a session with others speaking on related topics, or you might be part of a symposium on a more unified theme organized by yourself or someone you know, or you might be in a "poster session" where you and about ten to forty others put up your papers (all vaguely related) on bulletin boards and people can come by to talk to you about them. These meetings and conferences can be quite stimulating, and of course in social psychology they are also very social affairs.

Some social psychologists don't like writing as much as other aspects, but many find it the best part. Daryl Bem (whom you'll get to know in the next chapter) said:

> I enjoy writing. . . . I see myself as primarily a writer. I don't think I could ever make it doing fiction so I do the next best thing. . . . I'm a writer who speaks in the language of data. To bolster my argument, I'll do a study.

The Science and the Art

Jerry Singer describes how he felt about learning behaviorist research methods while he was in graduate school, and the contrast between that and social psychology research.

You may get a twist in the terms of how you did the cards for the rat in a transposition—maybe dark gray on top and light gray on the bottom—but the methods were theme and variation of standardized methods. . . . The social psychology we were doing seemed to be much more rambling and free. It was sort of the difference between a very strict technical actor who has a script and then goes through a set of stock (although very difficult) techniques in order to present the material, or a stand-up comic who's improvising while he is creating in front of an audience.

There is plenty of work and hard-core science to doing social psychological research. Even the stand-up comic comes off stage sweating, and even the social psychologist must be very precise and rigorous at every step. But it really does seem that social psychologists, as John Arrowood said, get paid for what they love to do. Like artists, they would probably be willing to starve in order to express their creativity. But so far, they are paid enough to eat!

Of course all science must be a means of self-expression and a source of pleasure or scientists would quit. It must simply be that different types enjoy different kinds of research. It is hard for us to say. We have always preferred the sort of science that lets you study anything, in any crazy way you thought you needed to in order to get at the truth.

In the next section we'll show you what we mean. Our main goal is to give you a description of one research effort in its entirety—an effort of our own, so we know it intimately. But the section also makes another point: at the time these studies were done, in the 1960s, some psychologists did say we were crazy, both because of our methods and because the topic "didn't belong in science." But very few social psychologists ever said that. With typical liberality they'd say, "Why not? It sounds like fun to try to figure out how people fall in love."

Studying Love, Step by Step

I suppose getting the idea was the most enjoyable part. My research on love began when Elaine and I fell in love. It was while I was in graduate school at Berkeley. We met in a T-group (naturally) which was part of a class in small group process taught by Hugh Coffey, who had studied under Lewin.

Since love was so much on my mind, I decided to study it, and by the time I was ready to do my dissertation, at the University of Toronto, I had already tried out several approaches. In one study I had people who were walking around with distorted glasses (in someone else's perception experiment) also rate their attraction to the person leading them around. This was to be a test of the effects of dependence. Not much came of that try.

I obviously needed more theoretical knowledge, to balance my personal, "practical experience." So for my dissertation, and out of my own desire to be better prepared to research this area, I set out to "review the literature." That meant a summer in Berkeley ransacking the University of California library for every serious book ever written on the subject of love (there were very few in 1969) as well as locating the very few research studies that had been done up to that time.

I was quite moved by reading the clear insights on love that were twenty-five centuries old. I also gained a great deal from the more recent, systematic analyses of this century. But the real joy came when I would find a book or article that clearly articulated something that had been my own intuition. I remember finding one obscure French monograph on passion that said exactly what I had been thinking, and more. Then there was a study of attraction and aggression that used such ingenious methods that I later adapted them to suit my own purposes. Each of these discoveries would keep me coming back for more, like a rat to the lever in a Skinner box. Each discovery also kept Elaine and me up half the night, talking about our own love in the light of these new thoughts.

Then came the fun of putting all the reading together into some semblance of order. It was a tremendously challenging, creative, and ultimately rewarding task. At the end, the wisdom of centuries, plus all sorts of other, tangentially related studies, all suddenly become an ordered understanding of something important to me. It was very satisfying.

By fall I had several clear ideas about what ought to generate love, or at least attraction, between people. All these ideas were based on the notion that there was more to falling in love than just the right combination of personalities (the main theory up until then). I and my obscure, passionate French friend thought that what also mattered was the circumstances under which people met. In particular, people are more likely to be attracted to someone they meet during unusual or "boundary-breaking" experiences, such as those involving power, mystery, isolation, or strong emotions.

But how to create such boundary-breaking experiences in the laboratory? I settled on the basic approach of having volunteer male subjects participate in a series of tasks with an attractive female student whom they had been led to believe was another subject for the experiment, but who was actually a student hired to play the part. This way her attractiveness and personality would be a "constant" and any differences between groups of male subjects would be due to the different tasks or circumstances I set up. After doing the tasks together, the subjects would complete questionnaires in which a few questions, hidden among many others, would ask the real subject how attracted he was to "the other subject." Also, the male subjects would write a story to be analyzed for attraction by counting the number of romantic and sexual words in it (an idea I got from reviewing the previous research literature).

As for the situations, I tried several tasks. To "operationalize" mystery, I gave only partial descriptions of a person they might meet and asked them how attracted they were to that person. The results were zilch.

But other ideas did work, and for the dissertation I settled on creating a strong emotional experience. It was "only simulated," like Zimbardo's prison study, but like that study, unexpectedly powerful in its effects. In the high-emotion condition, one of the scenes was that the subject played a captured soldier being tortured for information by the female subject. She would "torture" him by dripping "acid" (actually water) on him from an eye dropper until he would reveal his military secrets. I more or less directed, encouraging the subject to cry out whenever he felt the "acid" on his forehead, to try to feel as if it were actually excruciatingly painful, and to imagine that if it continued it would shortly burn through to his brain, killing him.

At the time, simulations were still a fairly new idea and I thought it would be hard to create emotion through role playing. I was wrong! The subjects' hands shook, they perspired, and when asked later, they all said yes, they felt *very* strong fear. As for my poor assistant,

several times when we were done for the day, I had to help calm
her down after "she had only pretended" to torture a half-dozen
people.

In the control condition, she and the subjects played the same
roles, except the fluid really was supposed to be water, which she
was using as part of a long, slow water torture and which at this
early meeting he would not find very bothersome.

Of fifty-two subjects, only one guessed that the female student
was actually our assistant. Our assistant never guessed that the extent
to which the subjects were attracted to her was what was being
measured. I was pleased with my directing, if surprised by its ef-
fectiveness.

With data in hand, I went to work on the statistical analysis. This
was relatively simple, just a matter of plugging numbers into a computer and waiting for the result to come out. But at the emotional
level, it was anything but simple. This was *my* Moment of Truth.

To my great delight, it worked. Those in the high-fear condition
did show, for example, significantly more desire to kiss my confederate (one of the key questions) and wrote more romantic and sexual
content into their stories. Looking at the details of these results, I
found that the situation had generated, quite specifically, romantic
attraction. Men in the high- and low-emotion situations showed no
difference in their answers to the questions "How much would you
like to have your partner in this experiment as a work partner?" and
"How much would you like to have your partner in this experiment
as a platonic friend?"

That study, together with the power study described in chapter
1 and my theoretical work, was my dissertation research (Aron,
1970). (Writing up my research and presenting it was an experience
in itself, full of sleepless nights, camaraderie, and major and minor
triumphs.) But these preliminary studies were just the first step. I
wanted to know more about love and attraction, and I especially
wanted to replicate these findings in a more realistic setting.

Fresh out of graduate school, I traveled west to Vancouver where
my friend and fellow social psychologist, Don Dutton, had just
joined the faculty of the University of British Columbia. We were
chatting one day, probably at Wreck Beach, about my findings and
where to do the next study, when Don remembered just the place

for arousing strong emotions—a scary suspension footbridge in a nearby provincial park. We went to see it.

This bridge was fear itself. It was about 400 feet of wobbly boards fastened to wire rope that swung in the breeze 100 feet above a raging river. (Later, just to be sure we were not the only cowards, we gave questionnaires to people who had just been on the bridge, asking them if they had felt anxious or tense out there. They had.)

Next there was the planning. Don, Elaine, and I talked for hours at our favorite Greek restaurant, thinking out all the details. We would have an attractive female student stand out at the middle of the bridge and stop each man walking over who looked between eighteen and forty and was alone. She would ask him to help her, right there and then, with a study she was doing for her sociology class "on creativity in beautiful places." If he agreed, she would hand him a clipboard and ask him to write a couple of brief stories based on pictures she would show him (essentially the same procedure used in the earlier laboratory experiments).

Then (we got really excited about this idea) when the man was done with the stories, she would tell him, "I'm sorry I can't tell you any more about the study until it is over, but—it will be over to-night—and if you want you can phone me to learn more about it." She would tear off a piece of paper and write her first name and phone number on it. Our prediction, hunch, and hope was that those who were more attracted to her would be more likely to call.

This still left several problems. What would be the nonemotional control condition? We went back and found another bridge nearby, built of heavy cedar beams and crossing a shallow rivulet. She could ask an equal number of men to fill out the questionnaire in the middle of this bridge.

Then there was the problem of the phone calls—who would actually receive the calls (not our poor, weary assistant). And also, how would we know on which bridge the callers had met her? We solved this by having the assistant use a different first name for the two conditions—switching names on different days of the project. The names we chose were Donna and Gloria, because she would be carrying Don's briefcase, which was inscribed "D.G.D."

Carrying out the study required one of us to drive our confederate to the bridge every day and stand by one end, unobtrusively watching to be sure everything went all right. About the only excitement to this part was the day the assistant came running to announce that a man was about to jump off the bridge. The park ranger and I talked him out of it.

Again, the statistics were simple. And again, the study worked. For example, of the twenty young men our assistant stopped on the scary bridge, eighteen telephoned that night. Of the twenty she stopped on the other bridge, only two phoned her. The results with the stories were also very clear.

Don and I wrote up the study, each taking parts of the article, and sent it off to a journal for publication. The editor liked the article, but he and two other reviewers said they had one reservation: could it be that the attraction was due to the men seeing our assistant as a "lady in distress"?

That was something we hadn't thought of, and a very good point. So we tried it again, back at the laboratory this time. We decided to create the emotion by repeating the part of Schachter's affiliation study that told students they would be receiving strong electric shocks. We even used most of the Gregor Zillstein script, name and all. Some of the time the subject expected to get shocked and thought that the attractive female "subject" would also be shocked.[4] Sometimes he was told that he would be shocked and not she, sometimes that she would be shocked and not he, and sometimes that neither would be shocked.

We reasoned that if the lady-in-distress theory was correct, the men would be more attracted to our assistant when they thought she would receive a shock, regardless of whether the man himself expected a shock. But if the idea of strong emotion, our original theory, was correct, the male subjects would be most attracted to the woman when the men themselves expected a shock, regardless of whether they thought she would be getting a shock or not.

An analysis of the data from this study found that the lady-in-distress theory, while a good idea, did not explain our results. But the strong emotion of the subjects completely explained them.

Now the article was accepted for publication (Dutton & Aron, 1974). And it has generated a good deal of exciting research since. Social psychologists especially seem to like it because it ties in with Schachter and Singer's results. Perhaps the subjects were experiencing an undifferentiated arousal caused by being on the scary bridge and thinking it was due to attraction to our assistant. This research effort has continued to be fun to discuss and tussle with for many years.

This Ticket Good for Any Ride

Social psychological research leaves so much room for freedom, and has so many aspects, that every social psychologist seems to passionately enjoy some part of it. Some glean the literature like Egyptologists putting together bits of papyrus from a tomb. Others like to put just the right question to nature, the one that will yield the unambiguous answer. Others like putting together the people, facilities, equipment, wording, and procedures, and refining the whole thing, until they have built a working drama which turns the researcher into a director, producer, writer, and perhaps supporting actor (the subject is always the star).

Then there are those who like actually carrying out the research, performance after performance, with all the camaraderie and excitement and good times that accompany any temporary, intense, meaningful endeavor. And some are addicted to that moment of truth—analyzing the results. Still others like broadcasting the results, sometimes literally, if the media get interested. Or putting it all together in a neat little package, working to get it published, and seeing it in print, one more addition to the total body of human knowledge.

But whatever part they like best, you can be sure they are enjoying it all. Because, for social psychologists, as Singer said, "Its just a satisfying feeling. When I'm doing it, things feel right."

Notes

1. Throughout this chapter the first person refers to Art Aron.
2. Actually, I was told to expect a fat "Jolly John" Arrowood, but walked into his office my first day at Toronto and found a very slim man with a refrigerator full of diet soft drinks at his elbow. He has never gained back all the weight he lost in the late sixties. That's self-control.
3. However, when we asked Stanley Schachter about this stage, he told us, "Those of us in the Group Dynamics group were there at the start." Since there was no literature to review, "we never got in the habit." But that's Stanley Schachter. Besides, in his published papers, his reviews of the literature show the same thorough attention, and ill-concealed delight, that's true of all the other details of his research.

4. Choosing "attractive" research assistants was a story in itself, one with at least one happy ending. Many years later, Don and the assistant in this study met again and are now very happily married.

7

"That's Just the Hypothesis. Wait till I Get to the Punchline."

I N social psychology, good theory tends to be a personal, passionate endeavor. This is probably true for all good science, as we'll discuss in the last chapter. But, as often seems to be the case, what is only a flavor in other fields tends to be a banquet in social psychology. The following example is a piece of history, a battle, and a drama all at once. And it is also a prime example of theory building in social psychology.

The Leading Man

Leon Festinger was the prize theoretician among Kurt Lewin's students and uncontested King of Social Psychology for twenty years after Lewin died. His reign only ended when he became bored and abdicated, taking up the study of perception first, and now "the history of humankind." But as Festinger tells it, he would have been just as happy from the start as a professional chess player.

> I grew up in the Depression. It didn't seem one could survive on chess, and science is also a game. You have very strict ground rules in science and your ideas have to check out with the empirical world. That's very tough and also very fascinating. (Quoted in Cohen, 1977, p. 133)

After having given up the hope of making a living at chess, Festinger tried studying physics and then other sciences. But he turned to psychology, and eventually social psychology, because "The impression I was left with was that here was a field that was scientific and had questions to be answered" (quoted in Cohen, 1977, p. 132).

Festinger has always been a central and controversial figure. Even in Lewin's *Quasselstrippe* he was "the most exciting intellectually . . . the most stimulating" (from our interview with Morton Deutsch). Festinger was also usually the leader of whatever faction was fighting tooth and nail with other views, while Lewin looked on with a "benign smile" and always made it come out right in the end.

For the most part, you either loved Festinger or you hated him. Elliot Aronson, who was one of Festinger's many successful students, first tried to avoid him as a new graduate student at Stanford. "Festinger had a reputation for being terribly difficult and harsh with graduate students." Finally Aronson was shamed into attending a seminar of Festinger's, which because of Festinger's reputation, almost nobody had signed up for. A friend of Aronson asked him why he wasn't taking this seminar with this "very bright guy." So Aronson agreed to attend. He was extremely impressed.

> It was the first time I ever saw a really brilliant research mind at work. Festinger had enormous confidence that he could do anything— look at the most interesting topics and examine them experimentally. That kind of intellectual flamboyance is remarkable and wonderful.

But it was also true, says Elliot, that Festinger

> was very impatient with sloppiness in thinking. He had a way of looking at you [if you slipped] that was a combination of impatience and sorrow—he really felt sorry for you because you were so dumb. . . . He didn't suffer fools gladly.

Festinger has always been notorious for irreverent remarks and behavior. After returning from a trip to the Orient he reportedly commented that "the Wisdom of the East is errant nonsense." (Though he did appreciate having learned to play the game of Go, a kind of Japanese chess.) Nor did he have the taste or talent for the kind of democratic leadership that Lewin had provided. Jerry Singer tells the following story:

> I was once on a committee which Leon chaired. We were planning a major conference and going back and forth about how to invite people when Leon said, "Tell you what, why don't we each suggest anybody we can think of who may even be topically appropriate? We'll put

the names on the board, then we'll eliminate them until we've narrowed it down to those we think should be at the conference . . .

Everybody concurred, names were suggested, and Leon stood up at the blackboard, writing them all down. Then when all the potential names had been exhausted, Leon said, "Okay, let's go through this. Number one. This person is not good because of" this, that, and the other thing. Zap. He scratches out the name with the chalk. "Number two. Here's a person that seems to be reasonable because his work's important and it fits this conference. I think we ought to keep this person for consideration." And he circles it. He goes through name after name, then comes to one that he says, "some people respect, but he's never done an experiment in his life and I think that this is totally inappropriate . . ."

But a very distinguished member of the committee interrupts and says, "Leon, I think we ought to consider this one further. He has a great following" and so on and so forth.

Leon nods very sagely and says, "You know? You're absolutely right." And as he's saying this, his hand almost automatically is just scratching out the name entirely.

Singer emphasized to us that the point of this story was that Leon was usually two steps ahead of everyone else—ready to act while others were still processing information. Festinger *would* listen to criticism, and change his ideas accordingly. But he could be caustic when he thought an argument was not well thought out. When asked about one famous critique of some of his work (a critique not altogether kind in tone), he immediately replied, "Yes—but that's garbage." When pressed, he proceeded to demolish it piece by piece.

Festinger earned the honored position he held. As Aronson recalls from his student years with him:

He's a genius. And geniuses are very rare. He had the quickest, most courageous mind I'd ever seen in my life. And he didn't worry about failure. He could shrug off failure. And just went for it. Very, very smart. And very courageous. A rare combination. Along with the fact he was very well trained by Lewin.

Singer also praised his tremendous ability:

He's able to think very directly about a problem without digression. He has a self-imposed intellectual rigor . . . he hits to the heart of the problem and he stays with it.

Schachter, who studied under Festinger after Lewin, called him "a *very smart* man." And Harold Kelley, another who knew Festinger first with Lewin, called him "the guy who, when you are writing, you most see looking over your shoulder."

But it was not just sheer brilliance. According to Philip Zimbardo, Festinger held his honored position because his personality was "charismatic." He "had the ability to attract bright people around him, and to inspire them with his brilliance."

Aronson describes another crucial aspect of Festinger's leadership that he remembers from his student years with him.

> Festinger, who I described as being tough, was also extraordinarily warm and sentimental. He could reminisce in a very warm, nostalgic way about Lewin. Mostly about the goodness of the man, the brilliance of the man, and the atmosphere that existed around him.

Festinger created his own version of the *Quasselstrippe*. Aronson remembers a lot of camaraderie among the students and Festinger. "We used to meet once a week over at Leon's house in the evening, drink beer, and generate ideas together in a constant, consultative atmosphere."

Elaine Hatfield, another former student of Festinger's, has a similar impression from her student years:

> He was a lovely person to work for. He used to make people in the outside world angry all the time because he was irreverent. I think they just weren't used to someone from New York, with a sort of New York, lower East Side fierceness. I think they took him seriously, when he just loved to say outrageous things. But he was always really kind to his students. He loved research. Yes, he was argumentative. I would train my students differently. . . . But I couldn't have had a better professor than Leon. I just loved to see him. . . . Students liked him so much that they all got together and tried to learn to play "My Yiddishe Mama" on mandolins and guitars because that was a song he liked a whole lot. . . . He did have all sorts of one-liners, sassy things he said to visitors. But he only picked on people his own size.

By 1957, Leon Festinger had already introduced several theories that are still among the most important in social psychology. But in that year his theory of cognitive dissonance was published (Festinger, 1957). Within one year it was the very center of American social psychology. And it stayed there for ten more years, because it was an exciting, simple, bold idea that explained a lot of human behavior. Even better, it did it in a way that seemed to fly in the face of common sense and of established thinking in the rest of psychology.

Festinger's cognitive dissonance theory says that people are uncomfortable when two beliefs they hold or a belief and something they have done are in conflict or "dissonant." In order to reduce this discomfort of dissonance, they are motivated to change either what they believe or what they do.

To demonstrate his point, Festinger did a study, with J.M. Carlsmith, a very bright undergraduate student of his at Stanford. This study is now so famous that it is known simply as "Festinger and Carlsmith." In the study (Festinger and Carlsmith, 1959), male subjects first spent a half-hour placing and then removing twelve spools from a tray (told to do so "at your own speed") while the experimenter sat with a stopwatch making copious notes on a pad. Then the tray was taken away and the subject spent the next half-hour with a board with forty-eight square pegs which the subject turned, one at a time, a quarter turn clockwise, and then another quarter turn clockwise, and then another, and another.

After they had done these very boring tasks, the experimenter would explain that the experiment actually had two conditions. In the other condition all the subjects were being told to do exactly the same tasks, except that first they were being told, by someone they thought was a previous subject, that the experiment was very enjoyable. This supposedly previous subject said things like, "It was a lot of fun, I enjoyed myself; it was very interesting; it was intriguing; it was exciting." Having explained the "other condition" (which really didn't exist), the experimenter continued:

> Is that fairly clear how it is set up and what we're trying to do? . . . Now, I also have sort of a strange thing to ask you. The thing is this. [Long pause . . . with . . . a degree of embarrassment . . .] The fellow who normally does this for us couldn't do it today—he just phoned in, and something or other came up for him—so we've been looking around for someone that we could hire to do it for us. You see, we've got another subject waiting [looks at watch] who is supposed to be in that other condition. (Festinger and Carlsmith, 1959, p. 111)

At this point the subject would be offered money to play the part of the "previous subject" who found it all very interesting and exciting. Half were offered $1.00, half were offered $20.00. Only three of the fifty-one subjects who were asked to help out refused. And all but three more actually carried out their job of telling the "next subject," a young woman who was really a confederate of the experimenter, that it was an exciting task. In fact the situation was rigged so that she would say that someone she knew had taken the experiment and had said it was not at all interesting and she should try to get out of it. In order to carry out the job they had been asked to do, the true subjects then tended to say things like, "Oh, no, it's really very interesting. I'm sure you'll enjoy it" (p. 206).

After all this, the true subject would be asked to complete some questionnaires about how interesting he had honestly found the experiment to be. Finally, the *real* experiment was explained.

The situation was intended to create dissonance between what the subjects initially knew from their experience (that the tasks were very boring) and their behavior (telling the woman that it was interesting). Furthermore, Festinger and Carlsmith predicted, on the basis of dissonance theory, that the group paid $20.00 would not suffer much dissonance because they would simply explain to themselves that they had lied a little because they were being paid so handsomely to do so. (In 1957 $20.00 was a *lot* of money for a ten-minute job.) But the $1.00 group would suffer much more dissonance, because they would have to ask themselves, in effect, "Why would I lie for only $1.00?" To resolve this, they would decide that they had not lied that much, that the tasks were not actually so very dull. On the final questionnaire, the $1.00 group would show a greater liking for the experiment than the group paid $20.00.

The results were beautiful. There was almost no difference in the ratings of how enjoyable the tasks were between the group paid $20.00 and another, control group who had just done the tasks without being asked to do anything special afterward except complete the questionnaires. But the $1.00 group rated the task as substantially more enjoyable.[1]

This result and the prediction on which it was based were revolutionary. So were the predictions and results of many dozens of other studies which came quickly on its heels. Elliot Aronson, who was Festinger's student, was one of dissonance theory's early champions. In fact, he is considered by many to be social psychology's outstanding experimenter. About dissonance theory's predictions, he told us:

> As a community we have yet to recover from the impact of this research—fortunately! You see, for many working social psychologists, these results generated a great deal of enthusiasm and excitement; but for others, skepticism and anger. Because, the finding departed from the general orientation accepted either tacitly or explicitly by most social psychologists in the 1950s: [that] high reward—never *low* reward—is accompanied by greater learning, greater conformity, greater performance, greater satisfaction, greater persuasion. . . . [But in Festinger and Carlsmith,] either reward theory made no prediction at all or the opposite prediction. These results represented a striking and convincing act of liberation from the dominance of a general reward-reinforcement theory.

Another radical aspect of the theory was that it forced psychologists to take mental events into account, something we said in chapter 5 was not at all acceptable at that time. Maybe *social* psychologists could be tolerated when they talked about thoughts or perceptions— but only as long as they stayed in their own domain and kept it in relation to groups or attitudes. To challenge the rest of psychology with a theory that might refute both reward theory and behaviorism was sheer impudence. As Tony Greenwald, who has written extensively about dissonance theory (for example, Greenwald & Ronis, 1978), commented to us:

> Now we understand that the truth is almost the reverse of those generalizations [provided by behaviorism]. The smallest incentive you can possibly use to get someone to do something is likely to be the most effective in getting the person to like the activity and keep on doing it. The theoretical reason for this is that in the adult human, particularly, reward does not operate by instrumental learning and classical conditioning mechanisms, but by cognitive dissonance or attribution mechanisms, whereby people arrive at explanations for their own behavior by taking note of the conditions under which they generate the behavior. So this is a cognitive understanding of the way incentives operate rather than a mechanistic conditioning law.

Festinger suggested another reason the theory was unpopular: "The image of Man that was portrayed was not very idealistic . . . dissonance theory certainly contains the idea that people are willing to delude themselves and to twist the facts" (quoted in Cohen, 1977, p. 139).

Whatever the reason, some psychologists were angry. For example, at a Yale colloquium an eminent social psychologist pointedly and conspicuously fell asleep while Festinger was speaking. And a Yale student remembers that the first thing he was asked to do as a graduate student was run a study intended to prove Festinger wrong.

Others (including some at Yale) felt that this theory, along with Schachter's work on anxiety and affiliation, had "put social psychology on the map." As Aronson said, "The theory was fertile as hell. All we had to do was sit around and we could generate ten good hypotheses in an evening . . . the kinds of hypotheses that no one would have even dreamed of a few years earlier."

For example, one counterintuitive prediction, verified in a study by Aronson (Aronson & Mills, 1959), was that people who underwent a difficult, embarrassing "initiation" into a group would be more attracted to the group than those who had endured a less painful initiation. Another verified prediction (Aronson & Carlsmith, 1963) was that children who did not play with an originally very attractive and forbidden toy, but under conditions where violation of the prohibition would have resulted in only a very mild punishment, would find the toy less attractive than if there had been a large punishment for violating the prohibition. (According to the dissonance theorists, the children in the low-threatened-punishment condition, in order to reduce the dissonance of not playing with the desired toy, decided, "I must really not like that toy very much after all.")

Yet another counterintuitive prediction of dissonance theory demonstrated by other researchers (for example, Ehrlich, Guttman, Schonbach, & Mills, 1957) was that after making a decision (for example, to buy a particular brand of new car), people will then act in a number of subtle ways to justify that decision to themselves (for example, spend more time reading advertisements for the car they bought). The logic is that because they had been considering several options before the decision, but have now chosen only one, the choice they make is dissonant with the other options they had been considering, so now they must reduce this "postdecision dissonance."

But as Aronson points out, predictions that are "nonsensical in one decade can become 'common sense' several years later—and even old hat and boring in a third decade" (1980, p. 15). By the late 1960s, social psychologists' love of the new and the nonobvious had many looking for an alternative to dissonance theory. A review of the literature at the time commented on the "imperialistic dissonance hordes" which had mellowed. "The youthful brashness of dissonance theory is [being] replaced by well-fed middle age" (Sears & Abeles, 1969). It was time for a new revolution.

Enter the Magician

In 1960, after receiving his bachelor's degree from Reed College in Portland, Oregon, Daryl Bem arrived at the Massachusetts Institute of Technology to study physics with a Woodrow Wilson fellowship and a reputation for independence and brilliance. Graduate students at MIT must take a minor, and they were encouraged to take it at nearby Harvard, in some subject unrelated to physics. "Everyone else I knew in physics was taking their minor in math. So I decided to take mine in social psychology." Before long he was spending more time at Harvard than at MIT. He has been a social psychologist ever since.

He actually finished his doctorate at the University of Michigan, where he was officially a student of Ted Newcomb (see the Bennington College study described in chapter 2). At Michigan Bem was an iconoclast and isolate. He never had an office near the other social psychology students or faculty. And he remembers that among them "there was a great rapport and group feeling . . . and I was always relatively peripheral. I got along with everyone. But I was pretty much a loner." This isolation could not have been helped by the fact that, while he deeply valued the personal friendship and support he received from Newcomb, he chose as his real mentor a Skinnerian named Harland Lane.

With this interest in behaviorism, Bem sounds more like Floyd Allport than any of the other early pioneers. When we asked him about this, he said, "Allport was one of the social psychologists that made sense to me when I read him . . . sort of a forerunner of behaviorism . . . the individualistic approach to social psychology." Until we'd told him, Bem had not known that Allport too had been a loner.

Bem is not quite the colorful character of legend that Festinger is. Nor has he ever occupied the position of revered leader that Festinger achieved. But neither is he dull. And he certainly knew how to attack the "well-fed" status quo.

For starters, Bem is an accomplished magician. Don Dutton reports that one evening after a conference several social psychologists were sitting together and Bem performed a number of card tricks. For his final act, Bem took a new deck, let everyone inspect it, and asked someone to pick a card and not show it to him. He then removed his coat and tie and shirt. On his T-shirt was printed the card the person had chosen!

His most famous magic trick was making the dominance of dissonance theory disappear. One social psychologist, John Touhey, recounts the excitement of the graduate students at that time:

> When Daryl Bem took all those ideas he took from B.F. Skinner (very loosely), gave them a symbolic interactionist cast, and reinterpreted dissonance theory—this was the major model of an upheaval in my graduate school days.

The upheaval was Bem's doctoral dissertation. As a social psychologist interested in attitudes, Bem set out to see if he could use Skinnerian principles to change attitudes. In what he calls the "brown bread study," he had residents at a home for retarded boys recite the statement "I like brown bread" and gave them a small reward. As a control, another group of residents just listened to a narrator saying "you like brown bread" and received the same total amount of reward, at the end.

The experiment "failed" from at least the obvious Skinnerian point of view—receiving or not receiving a reward right after hearing or saying the statements made no difference in attitude—but *both* groups showed a very substantial increase in brown bread consumption. This led Bem to "toy with the idea that self-persuasion is really a variant of interpersonal persuasion." That is, maybe it doesn't matter who says the words, as long as they are heard. Maybe we don't make as much of a distinction between ourselves and others as has been thought.

At about the same time, Lane had told Bem that "Skinner and I usually take the position that every person is really two people: the person behaving and the observer of the behavior."

This gave Bem the idea of merely describing a dissonance situation to subjects, so they could act as observer. Having described a situation, he would have the subject infer what the attitude of the person in the situation must be. Bem thought that people hearing a description of a dissonance situation, but not actually experiencing the supposed conflict, would predict an expected final attitude for the person described to them that was no different from the final attitude that was actually reported by those in the real experiment. In other words, living through the conflict was not necessary. The situations did not create a strong "motivation" to achieve some sort of "balance" or freedom from internal dissonance. Persons in both the real experiment and the observational version of it simply looked at the behavior they performed or had had described to them and said, probably quite calmly, "If I said that, I must have liked the experiment." Or, "If I said that, it was because I was paid a lot of money."

When Bem told his idea to Lane, "He bet me a strawberry soda that it wouldn't work—and I won the bet."

In one such study, Bem (1967a) merely described the Festinger and Carlsmith study, *from the subject's point of view,* step by step. He did not describe both conditions to each subject, but only the condition he had randomly assigned them to imagine.

The size and direction of the difference in questionnaire answers for the $1.00 and $20.00 conditions in Bem's observational version was almost identical to that of the original experiment!

Here was a revolution. It wasn't recognized immediately. Bem admits his dissertation was "virtually unreadable, it was so heavy with Skinnerian language." Even when he published his dissertation studies in the *Journal of Experimental Social Psychology* (Bem, 1965), they were still in the language of behaviorism and Skinner. But as he continued to write and speak about his idea, he found himself becoming increasingly cognitive.[2]

Bem believes that Harold Kelley's (1967) Nebraska Symposium paper on attribution, which included Bem's theory as an example, is what finally brought his work into the mainstream of social psychology. His own changing of his language must have helped a great deal as well. (It was one thing to attack social psychologists' favorite theory, but to attack their very language was too much.) With some practical advice from Ted Newcomb on how to go about it, Bem wrote an article (1967a) for the very prestigious and widely read *Psychological Review.* After two rejections, it was finally accepted.

This time his ideas did get a reaction. In Bem's own words, he had "attacked what was then King of the Hill, and the response was immediate." While there were many people in the wings who disliked dissonance theory, they had by now largely abandoned the fight, and for the next several years Bem stood his ground essentially alone, and with great vim and vigor, against the combined onslaught of Festinger's students and admirers. (Festinger himself had long since lost interest in the whole thing and was off studying perception.)

The first attack came from Judson Mills, who had been a student with Elliot Aronson under Festinger. Mills (1967) immediately published a reply pointing out that his own psychology students could not predict the results of Festinger and Carlsmith (thereby providing a quickie failure-to-replicate). But Bem (1967b) wrote back that Mills's students could not duplicate the result because the study had been described to them from the experimenter's perspective, not from what Bem held to be the subject's perspective.

But as that response was being dealt with, a more sustained attack was forming. Bem relished it: "A group at Yale and Duke were independently, without each others knowledge, trying to prove that I was wrong. . . . I was the one that told them about the other group. . . . Then they merged and the paper [Jones, Linder, Kiesler, Zanna, & Brehm: 1968] was published with several authors." He also recalls:

> When I visited Duke, Jack Brehm [another former Festinger student] said to me, "Well, our experiments are now complete" (this was before they were published) "and we have found it much easier to refute your position than we thought." And I, being still young and green behind the ears, trembled in my boots. I was scared to death.
>
> But then when they published it, I thought they had essentially made the same misreading that Judson Mills had made. So I sort of enjoyed the whole thing. I enjoyed making the rejoinders. And my perception is that I won.

Bem learned to stay quite mellow about the whole thing.

> Many of them seemed much more intense about it than I was. I thought it was kind of fun—after my initial trembling that they were going to smash everything I said . . . I was relatively relaxed about it.

Even his original hero, Skinner, was proud of him. Bem says,

Skinner loved it. Someone once asked Skinner in one of his lectures, "What about dissonance theory?" and B.F. Skinner said, "Well, Bem has proven dissonance theory to be wrong"—an interesting reading of it. That's what B.F. Skinner wanted to believe.

Peace At Last

When Bem says he feels he won, he quickly explains that this is only in the sense that his ideas became part of the dominant paradigm that eventually took over social psychology, that of attribution theory, while dissonance theory moved to the back seat. But as an understanding of certain phenomena, dissonance theory will probably always be with us. It works better than self-perception theory in some situations, and Bem is the first to admit it. There are also some points that self-perception theory cannot explain—for example, that physiological arousal occurs during some cases of dissonance.

These days Bem and Aronson, once warriors on opposing sides, both seem to approve, more or less, of a resolution offered by Russ Fazio, Mark Zanna, and Joel Cooper (1977). It says both theories are correct, but they apply in different domains. When there is a large amount of discrepancy, dissonance theory works; when there is a small amount, self-perception theory works.[3]

One reason for Bem's own receptivity these days to cognitive dissonance as an explanation for some phenomena is that he knows he has experienced it! He has letters to his parents from the times before and after he switched from physics to psychology in graduate school. "And the letters after the switch certainly show postdecision dissonance reduction. And that's not just self-perception. That had strong motivational and emotional content to it. So if you ask me, do I believe in dissonance theory—yes, I certainly do."

Perhaps the basic problem with dissonance theory for Bem was that he also experiences the self-perception phenomena he has described, and he experiences them in many situations that, before he came along, cognitive dissonance had been used to explain. Even other people who know Bem have commented on the fact that he seems to do things first, then observe what he's done and use that to understand what he feels—just the way he has described self-perception theory. When we brought this up to him, he said,

My wife [Sandra Bem, an influential social psychologist in the area of sex roles] could not possibly have made up self-perception theory because at the end of the day she'll say something like, "I'm feeling kind of depressed, I wonder why," and then she'll review the day's events to find out why. I'm much more likely to say, "Gee, I wonder how I feel? Well, today this happened and that happened. I guess I'm a little depressed." And that's self-perception theory. I tend to have very little access to my internal states and feelings. I've gotten better—nothing like marriage to help you have some access to your internal states and feelings.

And to soften the vehemence of a theoretical stance. But undoubtedly, now that social psychology is so focused on attribution theory, some new revolutionary is gleefully preparing to demolish the self-satisfied, attribution status quo.

The Joy of Theory—A Heritage

Social psychologists enjoy these battles, not so much for the skirmishing as for the insights that are pulled out of the field's brightest minds by this spirit of competition. And if the insights come from cooperation instead, which they do just as often, that's fine with everyone too. The point of this history of the dissonance and self-perception revolutions is that those involved were *openly and passionately* interested in the questions.

Like so many of the characteristics we have discussed, this rampant enthusiasm was modeled for later social psychologists by Lewin. Reportedly he could get so excited about ideas that when he was driving he would scare people nearly to death because he would take his hands off the wheel repeatedly to emphasize his points. Similarly, Dorwin Cartwright (1978) remembers Lewin, just a few months before his death, showing up late one night at Cartwright's house, bursting with excitement about some new idea.

When you love ideas, you find them everywhere. A school of theory about tension systems came from one of the *Quasselstrippe's* many visits to a Vienna café. Everyone would order coffee, then cake, then an hour later more coffee, then later more cake—and the waiter always remembered everyone's bill. But Donald MacKinnon (famous for his work on creativity) remembers that one night, a half-hour after everyone had paid, Lewin called the waiter over and asked him to write everyone's check again (reported in Marrow, 1969).

The waiter was indignant. "I don't know any longer what you people ordered. You paid your bill." And Lewin was delighted. He had wanted to demonstrate that a tension system had built up in the waiter, maintaining his memory, until the bills were paid. Many laboratory studies came out of this theory, called the Zeigarnik effect. It all was the result of a visit to a café, with Lewin's mind present and working full steam.

Others feel a calmer love for good theories, but it seems to be just as intense. For Hal Kelley,

> It's like the thrill people might have got in the olden days from putting together clocks—putting together these little parts, getting the mechanism running, and then seeing what it generates when it runs. That's really a lot of fun, and its part of what we do with theories—we take some simple assumptions, and set up some simple rules for interlocking them, we set that little system going, and the thrills are when it generates something you hadn't anticipated.

For others, theory represents independence. Self-assertion. Freedom. We've already caught this feeling from Bem, the Isolate, remaking the "in group's" social psychology until they *had* to notice. This feeling is well expressed by O.J. Harvey, a former student of Muzafer Sherif's (Harvey was the camp director in the Robber's Cave study) and well known for his theory of cognitive complexity.

> Rarely does a new fact shake the world. It's generally a capacity to look at old facts in a new framework. . . . Freedom is the ability to generate an option and act upon it. The ability to generate a new premise. We're trained and socialized . . . even in logic . . . we're always given the premise in society by someone else, and we're punished if we take premises that are deviant from the extant ones. We're called infidels in religion, we're called traitors in society. . . . But big discoveries come from the ability to take some new premise, some new perspective.

Or as John Touhey (a social psychologist whose work is in the more sociological, symbolic interactionist tradition) remarked about social psychology,

> It hasn't crystalized or hardened or limited itself to any narrow approaches. What I find wonderful about doing social psychology is

that I'm free to bring in ideas from all of the allied social sciences, and from the humanities as well. That's the charm, that to me is the cream—the fascination, the addiction, if you will—of modern social psychology.

This freedom, this love of wild ideas, is actively taught to each generation of social psychologists. The best example of this is Stanley Schachter, who emphasizes to his students that they shouldn't waste their time studying "bubbe psychology." Bubbe psychology is the study of what's obvious—the kind of finding that when you tell your grandmother (the Yiddish *bubbe*), she says, "So what else is new? They pay you for this?"

Aronson clarifies the point: "That doesn't mean we never test a bubbe hypothesis. But if all your psychology is bubbe, what the hell's the sense of being in the business?" It's more fun to show that the more people available to help, the less likely any one of them will help (Latane & Darley, 1970). Or that people will obey a white-coated scientist type even to the point of thinking they are injuring someone (Milgram, 1963). Or that the less you reward people to change, the more they change (Festinger & Carlsmith, 1959). Or that people can be made to say and even see the opposite of what is "obvious" to anyone (Asch, 1958).

We have had some fun doing this ourselves, with several theories. One resulted in the studies described in chapter 7: that people are more attracted to each other when they meet in a "boundary-breaking" situation.[4]

But the biggest fun for us has come from a theory of social influence via a nonmaterial but real social field, akin to the fields described by physics' quantum field theory and by Lewin. The idea comes from Eastern (Vedic) psychology (for example, Orme-Johnson, Dillbeck, Alexander, Van den Berg, & Dillbeck, in press) and a number of studies showing reductions in crime rates, accident rates, and the like that are apparently caused by small numbers of people practicing the Transcendental Meditation technique (see Dillbeck, Landrith, & Orme-Johnson, 1981). To study this experimentally, we (A. Aron & E.N. Aron, 1981a, b) moved groups of meditators in and out of high crime areas of cities and found the presence of people meditating together nightly in an area—just meditating, *doing nothing else*—yielded reliable reductions in that area's rate of violent crime of up to 30 percent. Meanwhile, in the peaceful and affluent suburbs where they usually meditated, while they were away crime rose as much as 30 percent.[5] Besides the practical implications, obviously part of the satisfaction of this research is that any theory to explain it has to go against "established psychology's" usual way of looking at the world.

When working on a new theory, one that flies in the face of common sense and established wisdom, the researcher may feel like an outsider. The ability to withstand that isolation, even enjoy it, while pursuing a new idea may be the essence of and the secret of at least some of social psychology's successful theory builders. On the other hand, the social support that social psychologists give to one another is also part of that success. For example, we have presented the idea of crime reduction through meditation and the social field to scientists of many persuasions, but social psychologists are always the most supportive, no matter what their intellectual reactions for or against. Rather than being threatened by an idea they do not fully grasp, they tend to understand and enjoy someone daring to try to turn psychology on its ears.

Elaine Hatfield has noticed the same tendencies among social psychology's theorists and wonders whether this tradition of seeing beyond the common sense and status quo, of standing one's ground enthusiastically when challenging what is accepted, and of supporting others who do so, may all result from the fact that numerous social psychologists were either members of ethnic or racial minorities or immigrants.

> They have a disadvantage in that they never have as much self-confidence as someone who has been in the majority group their whole life. But they have an advantage that far outweighs that—they see all sorts of things they are not supposed to see.

A Final Note

Whatever the reason for this tradition of exuberant theory, it seems to us that social psychology has been very productive of ideas. Every field seems to have its share of bright minds, but social psychology has nurtured those minds to do their theory building with an extra portion of independence and love of truth. And the world is better for it, as the next chapter shows.

Notes

1. The students were also asked to return the money afterward. Aronson, who was there at the time, remembers asking Carlsmith (who was personally conducting the experiment) about halfway through the study whether anyone had objected to returning the money. Only one subject had done so, someone in the $1.00 condition!

2. Bem was surprised by his growing use of cognitive concepts. He even included a long footnote in a 1972 summary of his work "apologizing" for his references to "inferential processes." But he found the cognitive language necessary. He told us that while it is possible to translate his ideas completely into behavioral terms, it is like trying to multiply and divide with roman numerals. He also feels it is a strength of his theory that it "survived the transition from a totally Skinnerian perspective to what to me was almost anathema in graduate school, which was a Heiderian phenomenological approach."

3. Interestingly, this dispute between a Lewinian-influenced and a Skinnerian-influenced theory was resolved with the help of a third tradition of social psychology, the social judgment theory of Muzafer Sherif (whom you will remember from the Robber's Cave and autokinetic effect studies). This theory explains very clearly just when a discrepancy is sufficiently large to require a dissonance explanation.

4. Since doing that research, we have extended that theory to explain a great deal of contradictory data about attraction under a theory that people love in order to expand themselves—and thus, for example, prefer opposites rather than similars (the previous and the commonsense theory) *if* they think they can maintain a relationship with the person (A. Aron & E.N. Aron, 1986).

5. We stopped replicating the experiment after we'd done it five times, when it became obvious that our credibility wasn't going to go up if we personally did it a hundred times. But the research keeps piling up—social field theory (E.N. Aron & A. Aron, 1986) may be the paradigm of the future.

8

"We Have a Dream. Still."

MUZAFER Sherif told us how he got into social psychology, or what he prefers to call it, the study of human relations. It was 1919 and the Greeks were arriving to occupy his native province in Turkey. Sherif was only fourteen or fifteen, but "I was always, even at that time, curious about seeing things for myself." So he went down to where the troops were disembarking.

> They came . . . and they started killing people right and left. The immediate thing that concerned me was that somebody else beside me was killed. . . . And I thought it was my friend and that I'd be killed too that day. Then the soldier . . . looked at me for a few minutes. He was ready to stab me. Then he walked away.
>
> That enmity that led people to kill each other made a great impression on me. There and then I became interested in understanding why these things were happening among human beings. I didn't know what profession I'd follow—the technical term for it—but I wanted to learn whatever science or specialization was needed to understand this intergroup savagery. I wanted to understand, and I devoted myself to studying human relations.

We have already seen how Hitler caused many social psychologists to direct their efforts toward understanding and preventing all that Nazism had been able to do to a nation of normal, upright people. Sherif's story is another verse in the same song. In fact, ask almost any social psychologist why he or she chose the profession, and they will tell you something like, "I wanted to understand how people could be so cruel." Or so uncaring. Or so stupid. Or they wanted to fight injustice, understand prejudice, help people get along with one another, prevent war. Or just help others live a happier, more loving, more fulfilling life. It is not true for every last one of them, but it is true for most. It is as though a large number of social psychologists have appointed themselves to be our species' self-improvement committee.

Here is another good example. We remember David Krech as the distinguished elder statesman of psychology who walked the Berkeley campus in the late 1960s with his cane and an air of great dignity. One of us took history of psychology from him, the other learned social psychology from his textbook, a thoroughly but subtly idealistic treatment. His reputation was as a hero of the loyalty oath struggle of the McCarthy era, and as a sympathizer with the late sixties' student "revolution."

During the Great Depression, however, David Krech (1974) was Isodore Krechevsky and he was running rat experiments at the University of Chicago, his umpteenth temporary, part-time, poorly paid appointment. Although he had published and was well respected as a psychologist, he was a Jew, which meant that even in the United States his chances were nil of winning one of the few regular university positions open at all during the Depression.

Until then, the studious Krechevsky had been largely oblivious to political and social events outside the laboratory walls. But by 1933 he could no longer ignore either his own mistreatment or the general state of joblessness and hopelessness in the world around.

Krechevsky, in his spare time, became a political activist. By 1935 he and some friends in Chicago got the idea that their social concerns might be shared by many other young psychologists (and it turned out by many senior colleagues as well). They formed an organization of psychologists "for the promotion and protection of research on 'controversial' topics . . . the authoritative interpretation of the attitudes of the socially-minded psychologists respecting important group conflicts, and the support of all progressive action that promises to aid in the preservation or creation of human values" (quoted in Finison, 1979, p. 30). They called their organization the Society for the Psychological Study of Social Issues, known as SPSSI, affectionately pronounced "Spissey."

While SPSSI was and is open to all psychologists, it has always been dominated by social psychology. As soon as it was formed it was joined by every major social psychologist of the time—Murphy, Newcomb, Floyd and Gordon Allport, Sherif, and of course Lewin and all his gang. Today more than three thousand belong, mostly social psychologists. According to social psychologist Marilyn Brewer, its 1984–85 president,

> It's an institutional identity for certain positions. . . . And its a place to which people refer certain kinds of questions. Psychologists say, "That's a SPSSI issue, let's see what SPSSI people say." . . . I don't think of it primarily as a political activist organization. There are occasions when it has been. But mostly its purpose has been to give all forms of support—from money to credibility—to people who want to do work which has social relevance.

Throughout the years SPSSI has been many things to many people, but it has always been a refuge for the politically aware social psychologist. With each new wave of social concerns in the United States, new generations of social psychologists have created or joined organizations to deal with it. During the early 1950s, young social psychologists interested in peace (a dirty word in those McCarthy, red-baiting years) formed the "radical" Research Exchange. Social Psychologists for Social Action was formed during the Vietnam era. Both these organizations were eventually incorporated into SPSSI. In the last few years new concerns, about women's rights, nuclear weapons, child abuse, and many other issues, have led to organizations of mainly social psychologists, new "committees" of SPSSI, or both.

SPSSI and its cousins is one outward manifestation of what we want to talk about in this chapter. The main point is that few social psychologists are ivory tower academicians. They care about the world. They want to make a difference. It is almost a universal characteristic of social psychologists.

Not that they agree on *how* to make the difference; that would be too much to ask. In particular, there is one main division among social psychologists, and we'll be discussing it: there are those who think the pursuit of "pure science" will best serve "applied" purposes in the long run, and those who believe it is important to work directly on applied issues. To lead up to that issue we must start where we always seem to have to start, with Lewin.

Action Research

Like Krech, Lewin started out just interested in psychology, pure and simple. But the events in his native Germany forced him to look around, and he gradually turned more toward social psychology.

He found racial and ethnic prejudice in the United States too, much as he loved the country and wanted not to see faults. Thus, by the early 1940s, he had already conducted the famous study of authoritarian and democratic leadership and was saying that it was not enough for psychology to understand behavior. "We must be equally concerned with discovering how people can change their ways so that they learn to behave better" (quoted in Marrow, 1969, p. 158). By the end of the war he had become committed to his often quoted dictum that there should be "no action without research; no research without action" (quoted in Marrow, 1969, p. 193).

Indeed, by 1946 Lewin had set up not one but two institutes to create and apply knowledge. One of them was the Commission on Community Interrelations, which he had persuaded the American Jewish Congress to fund as an institute to study and reduce intergroup tensions and prejudice. For its motto, he suggested the two-thousand-year-old saying from the famous rabbi Hillel:

If I am not for myself, who will be for me?
If I am for myself alone, what am I?
And if not now, when?

At the same time Lewin founded the Center for Group Dynamics at the Massachusetts Institute of Technology. The site was not accidental.[1] MIT focused on science and engineering, pure knowledge along with its application. Likewise, his new enterprise would integrate scientific theoretical and experimental social psychology with its applications, by creating "experiments in change."

[This goal of integrating the two] can be accomplished . . . if the theorist does not look toward applied problems with highbrow aversion or with a fear of social problems, and if the applied psychologist realizes that there is nothing so practical as a good theory. (Lewin, 1951, p. 169)

Chapters 3 and 4 featured some of the work done or inspired by the Center for Group Dynamics. Now let us look at some of the very practical problems Lewin took on for his Commission on Community Interrelations. While the goal was always to unite theory with practice, in this case practice tended to pay the bills: the CCI's funding came from the American Jewish Congress and they needed Lewin to make news by solving some real disputes if they were going to be able to continue to rationalize giving money to CCI.

The first problem CCI took on was an incident between Jewish and Italian Catholic teenage gangs, especially the latter's disturbance of Yom Kippur services at a synagogue in Coney Island. Lewin created a team to investigate, and it found that the attack was not so much against Jews as it was a venting of frustration due to lack of adequate housing, recreational facilities, and the like. So Lewin simultaneously worked with the mayor's office to improve conditions, and sent in a staff member, Russell Hogrefe, to work with the gang which had started the trouble. A year later, the gang was behaving in much more socially acceptable ways, and CCI's methods of changing the gang's behavior was later adopted by other agencies all over the country.

CCI also took on the problem of quotas for Jews in the admissions policies of universities. Conferring with American Jewish Congress members, Lewin argued that forcing discriminatory policies to be changed would eventually lessen prejudice. This would be a better approach in this case he thought, than relying on decreased prejudice to lead eventually to better policies. As a result of his advice, the AJC brought a suit against Columbia University's medical school and won. Lewin's point—that in the case of prejudice you can sometimes "legislate morality"—proved true years later, during and after the Civil Rights Movement, and was no doubt behind the thinking of the Equal Rights Amendment. (It was also a point which was at the core of dissonance theory.)

CCI also helped blacks get jobs at New York department stores. The stores argued that white customers would not buy from black sales personnel, but CCI did opinion surveys which demonstrated this was not true.

CCI disproved yet another myth too—that Jews always voted for other Jews. That study was done by Festinger.

Perhaps the most influential study from this period was done by Morton Deutsch and Mary Evans Collins (1951), on integrated housing.

It was a simple study comparing housing projects in New York

City with projects in Newark, its neighbor across the Hudson River. The housing projects were nearly identical except that Newark's were segregated, with blacks in different buildings checkerboarded around the project, while New York's project buildings were thoroughly integrated. The question was, did living in close proximity increase or decrease prejudice among the races?

Deutsch and Collins found that integration in these projects dramatically decreased prejudice. Those in the integrated buildings seemed to share a growing feeling of their common humanity. Hostility was being replaced by friendliness. Residents wanted to see their buildings even more integrated. In the segregated projects, whites were more prejudiced against blacks, wanted still greater segregation, and expressed more hostility even toward other whites. It had always been assumed that whites at least had to outnumber blacks for the whites to accept integration. But in fact, the best race relations seemed to be in a project that was 70 percent black.

The study bore much fruit, most of it sweet. While one pro-segregation group used it for evidence that integration should be prevented because otherwise the races would become too friendly (!), most public officials saw the point. Deutsch told us that because of the research, the Newark Housing Authority, where they did the study,

> found themselves under pressure from a lot of citizens groups to desegregate, and with the research results, and I think the basic willingness of the Authority, they in fact desegregated the housing project and no longer maintained separate buildings for blacks and whites.

In those postwar years everyone around Lewin felt the heady thrill of maybe being able to *do* something about social problems. From 1946 to 1950, fifty separate projects were carried out by CCI. Lewin's excitement about the whole thing was extreme even for him. It was a time of great creativity for him. In fact, some of Lewin's associates think his frenetic activity led to his early death in 1947. Not only was he still an active theorist, and social activist, but he was personally raising funds and maintaining public relations for his new institutes.

Gertrud Lewin, Kurt's wife, reminisced about this period:

> Kurt Lewin was so constantly and predominantly preoccupied with the task of advancing the conceptual representation of the social-psy-

chological world, and at the same time he was so filled with the urgent desire to make use of his theoretical insight for building a better world, that it is difficult to decide which of these two sources of motivation flowed with greater energy or vigor. (G. Lewin, 1948, p. xv)

From a Strong Trunk, Two Healthy Branches

Kurt Lewin's ability to integrate applied and theoretical social psychology was a feat that, so far, no one else has managed with the same adroitness. Even among his students and associates it was not the same smooth melding. Deutsch recounts the meetings of the *Quasselstrippe* at MIT:

> Lewin had different attitudes toward different people. Lippitt represented the applied aspect that Lewin was interested in, while Festinger represented a bright, theoretical, experimental kind of person. . . . There was a clash of orientations. . . . Not inevitably, but in fact there was such a clash. Festinger represented "science" and Lippitt represented "practice."
>
> [Lewin] encouraged vigorous debate. And there was a good deal of that. But he personally represented the fusion of a variety of interests. . . . So he would be able to somehow bring the positive strands from the conflicting orientations and weave them together into some unified position. And there was a certain . . . charismatic quality . . . he could pull things together and somehow everyone would feel enlightened.
>
> I do think there was a split after Lewin died. There was a group that got symbolized by Lippitt and Bethel and T-groups. . . . And then there was a group that got symbolized by Festinger and which represented a harder, experimental, theory-oriented approach. For awhile—ten or fifteen years—there was a kind of division in social psychology around that. But certainly in the last ten years, maybe even longer, that has no longer been true.

Other social psychologists we spoke with see this division as still not entirely healed. But everyone we spoke to, from those doing the most esoteric "pure" research on the thinking process to those conducting workshops on international peace, agreed that they want social psychology to have important practical value. The differences were mainly one of strategy.

To be Objectively Compassionate or Compassionately Objective

A number of social psychologists believe that the most important thing they can do to contribute to the betterment of human kind is to do the most purely theoretical, experimental research possible, so that they will discover principles that can be broadly applied. For example, Lee Ross emphasized:

> I think that the classic experiments that have contributed to theory development are more useful to the applied researcher than any particular applied study that has ever been done. . . . Part of it is that most applied research by its very nature has a degree of specificity about it that makes it not terrifically helpful in the way you think about the next situation. A classic theoretical study may be more relevant to the next thing you do than the last applied thing you do.
>
> Theoretical social psychology influences the model we have of human beings . . . situationism—why people are difficult to change. I can't imagine anything that's of more fundamental applied significance than the way you think about man.
>
> If you want to understand why social change has been so much harder to accomplish than all the applied psychologists thought it would be, the answers are to be found in theoretical social psychology, not in probing through the notes of applied psychologists. . . . But applied social psychology also keeps teaching dramatic lessons to theoretical social psychologists. It sort of says, "If you didn't get what you expected in the lab, stupid, look what happens in the real world."

Russell Fazio, whose work on cognitive processes is very much theory-oriented research, comments,

> I've always viewed our field as one that was primarily concerned with basic research and the establishment of theories and models. But I don't have any doubt that if we continue to build this theoretical foundation, we'll be able to apply it if we want to.

What you are hearing is a caution. Traditionally science is "pure." Physics doesn't worry about whether its discoveries will help space travel or the energy problem. Those problems are left to be solved by engineers and inventors—the people who apply science. Scientists fear that if they limit their thinking to what is needed at the moment, not only will they not make the type of basic discoveries which have in the past proven most fruitful, in the long run, but they won't be as objective, being in someone's pay, or focused on some one group's problem, or out to prove an ideological point.

Still, this caution overlies a continuous concern in social psychology for relevance, a concern for people. From many of the social psychologists we talked to, we could hear the constant struggle between the desire to help and the desire to be the *most* help, with solid knowledge and not wishful thinking.

An example is Marilyn Brewer's work on desegregation and cooperative learning. When asked about the practical value of the research she does, she was quick to defend its "pure" aspects.

> I'm strongly committed to the idea that understanding basic processes is the best route to real problem solving in applied settings, ultimately. And I strongly believe that problems should be defined in a broad way. That is, one shouldn't think of desegregation and prejudice as a specific problem to black-white relations in the United States today. But rather, one should look for a broader class of problems. I think, however, that when we design and think about basic research, it's important that we have in mind the problems that we are ultimately aiming to do something about. I think too much basic research has gotten too far away from any real connection with what's out there needing solutions.

Dalmas Taylor at the University of Maryland probably expressed the situation best, as well he might: he is a black social psychologist, specializing in self-disclosure processes and interpersonal attraction, but also with a strong personal and professional interest in the topic of discrimination and prejudice.

> The problem is that when you are involved in studying something, it requires a certain amount of objectivity and detachment. When you are involved in pursuing a remedy, there is less objectivity and a great deal of attachment. So you essentially end up wearing two hats, playing two different roles. I think that can be done, but it's very difficult. So occasionally I have advocated that the practitioners of social psychology not be the same people who generate the data or the findings. But I've modified that over the years, consistent with the discipline itself recognizing that the very selection of hypotheses and the paradigms that we use contain values, either covertly or overtly, and at any point along the line there's a certain amount of subjectivity. What we have is a series of methodological strategies that mitigate against our biases, and I think they perform a sufficient check and balance to let us play this dual role with less concern and less error.

If you look at the social scene in terms of what psychology has contributed by way of application, you see that some things get to the applied stage at a level and in a way that is almost divorced from the original motivation to pursue the topic, and others start out with an interest in solving a problem or making an application. My sense is that we have seen more applications from the former than the latter.

I am a minority, so I come to this with a sensitivity of someone who is a member of an oppressed, disadvantaged, and excluded group. I have been keenly interested both personally and professionally in eliminating the factors in our society that perpetuate prejudice, racism, and discrimination of any kind. I'm just committed to trying to make a change in institutions and in people. I've been involved in social responsibility in investment and the advocacy of economic boycotts of South Africa, and so on.

Some of this obviously goes beyond anything that our data inform us of, but that's the duality of being a professional who cares about these issues and being an individual who has a personal commitment to social change.

Still, what has been most personally satisfying for Taylor is not the application of his expertise to particular problems, but "providing a conceptualization and explanation of the dynamics of prejudice and racism that in some ways challenges the status quo." Once again we hear about the love of theory and the value of theory, even for solving concrete problems.

Getting the Fruit off the Branch and into the People

The problem, of course, is that if most social psychologists do pure science, who is applying all these findings to the problems that they all agree they want solved? Chemical companies apply chemistry, oil companies apply geology, but who applies social psychology? Some ideas are used by advertising and opinion pollsters, but much of it would be best used, expecially in the opinion of socially concerned social psychologists, in public agencies and institutions like government, schools, services for the disadvantaged, rehabilitation settings, and so forth—institutions that often lack the personnel to find out about or apply social science theory and findings to their problems.

For that matter, even the brightest practitioners and social policymakers tend not to know about social psychological findings, probably couldn't understand the jargon if they did read the research journals where the findings are hidden, and certainly would have a hard time seeing any practical implications of "the fundamental attribution error" or "cognitive dissonance" for their own policy or problem area.

Not surprisingly, many social psychologists believe that if they want to see their work applied, they will have to apply it themselves. For example, Don Dutton (see chapter 6) is now studying the effect of misattribution of arousal on family violence. Elaine Hatfield, perhaps the foremost researcher in the area of love, has an active marital therapy practice, where she directly applies the results of her own and others' research. John Gottman, whose research on marital communication you read about in chapter 4, has helped create marital communication training programs based on his work. O.J. Harvey, one of the researchers on the Robber's Cave study, has since worked on applying his theories of cognitive flexibility and belief systems to education.

Another approach to getting ideas applied is to make social psychological research so dramatic and obvious that the applications can't be missed. This was Phil Zimbardo's strategy with the Stanford prison study described in chapter 6. He used his very clear, relatively straightforward findings to try to persuade correctional authorities and other public officials to make changes in the prison system. Yet another such vivid demonstration was the Sherifs' Robber's Cave studies of intergroup conflict and conflict resolution.

Last but not least is the approach of teaching. Social psychologists are, after all, usually professors. During their career they may teach many tens of thousands of students, the vast majority of whom will not become social psychologists, but will be in a position to use social psychology personally or professionally. Teaching is obviously an important opportunity to point out the practical implications of theories.

The Well-Trained Mind Bears Fruit

We have suggested there are two branches to this tree of strategies for expressing social concern, a pure science branch and an applied branch. But it might be more accurate to say there are many branches. Or better, a continuum of branches, bearing social psychologists of all types, from those not at all concerned as professionals with any practical implications of social psychology; to those who are concerned but feel pure research and theory serve humankind best in the long run; to those who are also both concerned and agree that pure science serves best *but* make an extra, personal effort to get the pure science applied (we just finished describing that branch).

But there is one more limb to the tree, the branch of direct, applied, or "action research." Applied research uses the theories, and especially the methods of social psychology, to study and solve specific social problems. In fact, maybe the best way to describe this approach is to say it uses the social psychologist's mind as its tool, a mind that has been trained to look at behavior in unique ways. The applied researcher takes as his or her topics, not theoretical issues, but questions about how to solve specific problems in a real, struggling, social world. The studies done by Lewin's CCI are a perfect example.

Many social psychologists have offered themselves as consultants or advisors in this way. Some have private consulting practices where they help individuals or organizations. Others tackle broader social problems, like child abuse or addictions. But they all tend to make important contributions, just because of the perspective they bring to the problem. When Don Dutton began working with battered women's groups, for example, he was very impressed by how well social psychological theory and methods had prepared him to be useful "out in the world."

Another good example is Daryl Bem, the magician who developed self-perception theory as an alternative to cognitive dissonance theory. Like most social psychologists, Bem entered the field because he thought it was a way to help the world. Remember how he started out in physics at Harvard? The social psychologist who changed his mind was Thomas Pettigrew, who was teaching a course on race relations and had Freedom Riders up from the South to talk about the Civil Rights Movement. This greatly renewed Bem's interest in social psychology and brought him "into the fold."

These days Daryl and his wife Sandra Bem are busy applying social psychological methods and ideas to a number of applied projects, in addition to continuing their more theoretical work. Opportunities come up particularly in her area, sex roles, in which she is one of the leading researchers. Daryl described several cases to us:

We were asked by the Equal Employment Opportunities Commission to demonstrate that A.T.&T.'s advertising practices were perpetuating the segregation of jobs by always showing operators were female and linemen were men. We demonstrated the effect of that in a very simple study. And we won the case. We've done that three times in three different contexts. We consulted for the Highway Patrol in California—there are now women patrol officers. I have the feeling that it's the methods we apply that make the difference. But the results of the studies have the direct effects.

You recall Elliot Aronson, the former student of Leon Festinger who has earned a reputation as one of the outstanding experimentalists in the field. As a young assistant professor at Harvard, Aronson met one of the most senior members of the department, Gordon Allport, Floyd's brother. Gordon Allport had a strong sense of social commitment. For years, Aronson had always thought, like Festinger, that it was enough to do the research and let someone else apply it. But he remembered Allport telling him that unless you apply the knowledge yourself, no one else will. That thought nagged at Aronson, so about fifteen years ago he substantially broadened the focus of his career.

He had been doing experimental work exclusively, on interpersonal attraction and self-esteem, at the University of Texas, when he became aware of problems in Austin's schools because of desegregation. In some schools students of different races were staying particularly separate and hostile to each other. This tended to lower the self-esteem of the minority race students, thus hurting their classroom performance and education (and their self-esteem still further)—hardly the intent of desegregation. When violence finally broke out, Aronson got involved and was permanently changed by the experience.

My interest in self-esteem made it easy for me to jump into the school system when there was a problem—when there was a crisis there because of desegregation. But my actual involvement happened by accident. Austin was being desegregated and had riots. One of my former students was the assistant superintendent of schools for Austin, and he had heard me say many times in lectures how applicable this stuff is, so he thought of me to help solve this crisis. Then, once I'd tasted the experience of actually solving a crisis, Gordon Allport's influence became vivid. The laboratory seemed dull after that. Once we got significant results, instead of looking for another hypothesis to test in the laboratory, I was looking for another crisis to solve.

Essentially what Aronson did was apply the lesson from Robber's Cave. Do you remember what finally stopped the war between the Eagles and the Rattlers? A superordinate goal. Aronson decided that the goal for students is to learn. So he developed the "jigsaw class-room" (Aronson & Bridgeman, 1979), a method that forces students to cooperate in their learning.

Students meet in six-person learning groups in which each has one part of the written lesson and teaches it to the others. For the group to get the whole lesson, all have to be allowed to present and everyone has to listen to everyone else, regardless of race or ethnic background. Evaluations of the program show that it greatly increases participation by those previously excluded, obviously, and also raises self-esteem, liking for school, positive inter- and intraethnic perceptions, and empathy. Members of minorities also get getter grades.

While still an experimentalist, Aronson is now also involved in using social psychological knowledge about attitude change and social cognition to get lower socioeconomic households to make use of energy-efficient technology which is available to them free, but which up to now most have not adopted.

All in all, he feels the focus of his excitement has shifted from the *process* of research to its *outcome*, to the changes research can make in society.

> The whole idea for me now is to take research beyond the demonstration phase. Since 1971 I've spent a lot of my time in the office of school principals, trying to get them to understand why the jigsaw classroom would be useful in their schools—and failing more often than succeeding. I don't enjoy that process very much. But the beauty of jigsaw is not that it discovered something new. The beauty of jigsaw is that it packaged some knowledge in a way that works (the evaluations are superb) and that it is easy to use.

Another beauty of the jigsaw classroom for Aronson is the knowledge that it has made a difference in people's lives. "I still get letters from some of those kids in the classrooms, ones who are now in law school or in medical school, but who say they never would've gotten beyond the eighth grade if it hadn't been for that jigsaw experience."

As a result of his experiences applying social psychology, his viewpoint on social psychology's role in social change has changed markedly.

> I obviously think it should be a lot stronger than it is now. There should be social psychologists in high level positions in government. I think we have a lot to offer.

He seems to be right. Consider another example—Herbert Kelman—who is merely trying to use social psychology to maintain world peace.

Kelman told us he was excited by social psychology as an undergraduate, and decided he wanted to study with Kurt Lewin when he heard him lecture at his college. But by the time he was ready to enter graduate school, Lewin had died. Nevertheless, throughout his career Kelman has worked closely with many of those who studied with Lewin, and has maintained an action-research perspective.

Kelman did his graduate work on attitudes, however, and is well known for his "functional theory of attitude change." Looking back, he thinks that this rigorous "pure science" work gave him enough prestige and credibility to go ahead and do what had always been most important to him: research that makes a difference in the world.

He was a major founder of the Research Exchange on the Prevention of War and of the *Journal of Conflict Resolution*, was instrumental in getting the Society for Psychological Study of Social Issues to set up a committee on international relations, and is widely known for a SPSSI-sponsored book he edited, *International Behavior: A Social Psychological Analysis*. Most inspiring is his ongoing work with international workshops on interactive problem solving. He described them for us:

> The main idea is to provide an opportunity for people involved in a conflict to engage in the kind of interaction with each other that parties in a conflict usually can't engage in. Interaction in which they talk freely because the whole event is very, very private. Usually parties in conflict are talking for either their constituencies or for third parties. They don't talk to each other, and what's even more important, they don't listen to each other.
>
> Essentially we try to get them to talk about the conflict analytically, rather than the typical blame-defend framework. . . . We don't minimize the significance of people's perception of their rights. But we

try to get the parties to . . . express their own concerns, their basic needs and their basic fears, and to listen to the other's concerns—and then start asking questions about how can we find a solution that would be responsive to both sets of concerns simultaneously. That leads into a problem-solving stage.

Kelman has done most of his workshops with Palestinians and Israelis. Some have been with Egyptians and Israelis and with Greek and Turkish Cypriots.

The whole effort here is designed not just as a learning experience for the participants but as a contribution to the larger political process.

An example would be a workshop in which Palestinians come to the point where they can see that, for the Israelis, Zionism is a positive concept, that it is an expression of national liberation. They don't become Zionist. They still see it as inimical to their own interest. But they begin to understand that the meaning of Zionism isn't exhausted by the destruction of the Palestinians. And conversely, Israelis begin to understand what the PLO [Palestine Liberation Organization] means to the Palestinians. Again, they don't become supportive of the PLO. But they begin to see that the PLO is not just an agency dedicated to the destruction of Israel, but it is also a movement of national liberation and self-expression for the Palestinians. That Palestinians who identify with the PLO do so for positive reasons.

This then leads to the next step. It is possible for an Israeli to be Zionist and for a Palestinian to be a supporter of the PLO and yet be interested in peace. In order to have peace your enemy doesn't have to abandon his ideology, his commitment.

Mostly Kelman has worked with people who have influence in the decision-making process, sometimes even parliamentarians or party leaders, who are not top leaders. Kelman says,

Top leaders are not actually the ideal candidate. In order to involve themselves in the process they have to be able to play with ideas. . . . Top decision makers can't just toy with ideas. They are constantly aware that once they say something, it becomes a political reality.

Kelman knows the conflicts he's worked on are still ongoing. But he also knows that some ideas that have come out of these workshops have reached decision makers and influenced their decisions. The changes have been small, but he sees an impact. And he finds personal satisfaction:

> I'm using everything that I am and that I have. Whatever knowledge and skills and experience and credibility I've built up over the years— I'm utilizing all of it in trying to make a contribution to the resolution of international conflict.

That seems to be fairly concise description of a fulfilling career. Social psychologists seem to have a lot of such careers, perhaps because so many of them have devoted their lives to trying to help others while simultaneously using their minds to their utmost, with chutzpah and daring, in a cooperative (or playfully competitive) spirit with other bright, sociable people. Whether they choose to pursue pure research with the faith that deep knowledge best serves humankind, or they take their research out into the schools and social battlefields and find applications, or they use their minds as tools in applied settings—social psychologists generally show a deep concern for others.

We asked Morton Deutsch to describe what kind of social psychology program he organized at Columbia Teachers College when he went there in 1963. His answer sums up this chapter very well:

> I wanted to create tough-minded but tender-hearted students . . . people that would be sharp and critical and would know theory and know research methods. . . . But I wanted them also to have a tender heart, to be concerned with social problems. . . . Science is very important. But science without a heart can be destructive. And a heart without a mind is not very valuable. So I think its very important to have both.

In most of the sciences it has taken some hard lessons for scientists to see that they must allow hearts to be involved if they want the application of their work to have only positive influences. Sometimes it is easier or less unpleasant to ignore one's role in the bigger scheme of things. But that is something that is prohibited to social psychologists by the very nature of what they study. They are constantly reflecting on their own role in their discipline and in society, as we shall see in the next chapter. Does a tender heart make one more self-reflective? Or does self-reflection soften the heart? Or maybe they are the same thing.

1. Accident apparently helped a little. Supposedly Lewin would not have minded locating in Berkeley either, with its warm winters and congenial social and political climate. But the proposed center's letter of acceptance from Berkeley came two days too late.

9

"We Are the World."

WE have reached the last chapter. Looking back, you have met people, social psychologists by profession, who are caught up in the excitement of sorting out an issue, often very fine points of an issue, yet who keep a very broad vision of their purpose. At their best, humans are like that—self-aware. They observe and reflect upon their personal and collective history and struggle to predict and improve on their behavior. In fact, if we look back over the last eight chapters, not only can we see social psychologists, but ourselves as human beings.

What is so special about us humans? We can think especially well; we can hypothesize and then imagine results and visualize alternatives. We can mentally reconstruct the past and project consequences into the future. We have curiosity and spend a lot of time just exploring, playing around, and "having fun." We are aggressive, perhaps to a fault, and full of chutzpah. We use language, maintain complex hierarchies of internal representations, delay gratification, and we can love. We feel connections and commonalities between ourselves and others—other people, other species, other nations. The whole universe when we're warmed up to it. We feel empathy and want to help when others are in trouble. Above all, we are very, very social. We can't survive without one another.

All these human qualities also pertain to social psychologists as we have described them in these chapters. In fact, we could say that the paradigmatic social psychologist is just a human being with a bit more of many of these same qualities. This is not to say that social psychologists are the ideal humans, but they do point us in a good direction. In particular, they are focused on one area which seems to be our main human weakness: our relation to society. A lot of people are saying today that if we as a species are going to make it into the next century, we are going to have to get control of ourselves as a group. Certainly no one wants a nuclear war, yet collectively we have somehow prepared for one. Somehow society influences us but we don't influence it. We need to figure that one out.

That means self-reflection. And it seems to us that this may be the trait that most predominates within social psychology, at all the levels where we humans need to reflect—on ourselves as individuals, on our behaviors in groups, and on our role in our world. This chapter discusses the ways in which social psychologists are already engaged, to an unusual degree, in these three kinds of self-reflection.

When we started this book, we didn't expect to end it this way. But when we talked to social psychologists, and we asked them what characteristic sets social psychology apart from other areas of psychology or other social sciences, we kept getting a similar, unexpected answer—social psychologists are more "self-questioning," of themselves and their field and the direction their society has taken. Let's begin to explore this characteristic at the personal level.

A Mirror Held Up to Themselves

Almost every social psychologist we spoke to did not enter college intending to become a social psychologist. (How many people have even heard of social psychology?) Many did not even enter graduate school with social psychology on their mind. In this book we've seen that the field is populated by converts from English literature, physics, law, engineering, art, theology, chemistry, medicine, and you name it. They also slipped in from other areas of psychology, ranging from clinical psychology to animal learning. All these people came into social psychology because, unlike their fellow students who stayed in law school or seminary or what have you, they started questioning themselves about what they were doing. Think back over them: Festinger and Bem both began in physics but liked the issues in social psychology better; Lewin was interested in more general psychology, especially perception and learning; Heider slipped in from philosophy. At the outset of each person's career there was a sort of self-selection in favor of self-questioning.

Furthermore, while anyone may question their future plans, these people questioned *and* changed direction, making them unusually flexible, and perhaps also a bit impulsive and inclined to follow their hearts. As we have seen, a great many were looking for a place to express a deep-seated desire for doing something about the world. Others were excited about the enterprise of understanding human beings through scientific research. But it was rarely a drifting into social psychology; more often it was a self-reassessment. We especially enjoyed one story about this process, from Phil Zimbardo. He feels now that he was "practically born a social psychologist." But it took a fortuitous prod and some soul searching for him to see it.

[At Yale] I ran rats for three years. I was a rat man. The guy I was working for committed suicide. I applied for his grant. . . . I continued to do the research, even though originally I hated it. . . . another graduate student and I did a study which was published in *Science* . . . I was analyzing some of the data after it was accepted, running some other analyses. And Bob Cohen [a social psychologist doing work in dissonance theory] was sitting there. I guess I had had one course with him. And he asked me what I was doing. I got all excited describing the study—the effects of caffeine and chlorpromazene on the sexual behavior of the adult male rat. And he did a number on me. He said, "Could you look out the window and tell me what you see?"

I thought he wanted me to see if his bike was there. I said, "I don't see anything." He [repeated the question] . . . I said, "Well, there are some people."

He started saying, "Well, what are they doing?"

Again I kept thinking that they were people that he was waiting for. I started describing what they were doing. Then he just said something like, "Don't you think it would be more interesting to know what they were doing than to know what the rats are doing? Do you really care about the rats?"

It was one of those things. At first I was offended and then later I thought about it. I said to myself, he's right—that's really why I'm here, that's what I was interested in when I started out—people. I'd put on my application that I was interested in race relations, and there I was studying rats.

This self-reflection often seems to continue throughout social psychologists' careers. Remember the story of how Lewin showed up late at night at Cartwright's house with a new idea? The insight he'd come to discuss was one that meant "he would have to make a

fundamental revision in his entire theoretical approach," and Cartwright still remembers "how surprised I was that anyone could be
so pleased upon discovering a basic flaw in his own work" (Cartwright, 19178, p. 179).

Social psychologists seem to be constantly seeking new and more
interesting, more significant, or just more fruitful approaches to their
work. Or whole new topics. Schachter is famous for his broad range
of topics—everything from emotions to smoking, affiliation to obes-
ity. We saw that Bem was quite willing to agree to the validity of
dissonance theory—after spending several years attacking it. Aronson switched from a highly theoretical career to a highly applied
one. Festinger left social psychology altogether. Many, many major
figures in social psychology have made dramatic changes in direction
at several points in their careers. They look at what they are doing,
they question, and they act on what they see.

A Mirror Held Up to Their Discipline

People in most professions would not publicly challenge the very
assumptions of their discipline as social psychologists do constantly.
Is it relevant? Are we all wasting our time? Are we honest with
ourselves? Are we throwing away the public's research funds? (You
won't hear any other field ask *that* out loud.)

The major psychology journals regularly publish articles by social
psychologists raising questions about the fundamental value of what
the field is trying to do or the way it is doing it. This is not just a
few debunkers. Rather, it's the tip of the iceberg of an often agonizing
existential questioning of the worth of careers that many have in-
vested most of their adult lives in constructing.

In the early 1970s social psychology went through what is generally known as The Crisis. This period was an orgy of collective
self-criticism, in which various authors argued that the "problem"
with the field was that it was not applied enough. Or that it was
not methodologically sophisticated enough. That it was too caught
up in small, trivial studies and ignored the big questions. Or that it
was constantly flitting from big question to big question without
following up on the little details. People were having too much fun.
Or not having enough fun. Or social psychology was too American,
too individual-oriented, or too mechanistic. Or it was unethical in

its research, or misguided in its attempts to be value-free and universal. And on and on and on.

Looking back at the history of the field, we see this crisis as an unusually strong example of what has been an ongoing process. Today, although the crisis has passed, there is still no shortage of internal criticism. Indeed, many of those we interviewed were discouraged with where the field is now and where it seems to be going. These people were not only criticizing other people, but feeling responsibility themselves for the flaws they were eagerly cataloging.

Fortunately, as in the case of their personal self-questioning, this collective mauling seems to result in changes. Most of those we interviewed sense an improvement since the crisis, that while much more could and should be done, there is reason for optimism. And of those who complained most vociferously about the state of the field, they were often doing work themselves that belied their complaints. Some said the field had lost its spirit and excitement. But when we asked them what projects in their career had been most satisfying, it was always their current one. Others said the field still was not doing enough about social problems. But these people were actively pursuing research and action that was, indeed, making a real difference. Those who felt the field was too mechanistic (the symbolic interactionists) were doing significant work showing social psychology how it could be nonmechanistic. And so on.

At the end of our interviews we asked, "Over and above the other things you've talked about, is there anything you would want to tell someone about this field if they were considering entering it?" One said he'd ask, "Have you considered art or music?" Others pointed out that the field is tough, and only those who are bright, creative, and self-motivated will find a comfortable home in it. Several emphasized the value of getting a broad education—studying the natural sciences and humanities, reading Dostoyevsky and Shakespeare. But the main response was that this is a field like the American frontier: it offers unlimited opportunity, wide vistas, and a chance for any enterprising young man or woman to build an intellectual "empire." It is a field where new and radical ideas are unusually welcome; where theories and methods of study can be borrowed from any field, from physics to drama.

What was most striking about the answers to this question, however, was the readiness with which everyone could answer it. They had all obviously spent considerable time reflecting on the nature of the field and observing it as an outsider might. They were very able to stand back and verbalize what the field was, in its essence, to them. And they were eager to pass their observations and reflections on to anyone willing to listen.

A Mirror Held Up to the World

While the rest of psychology—and the human race—has tended to think of humans as individuals, social psychology has studied the connection between individuals and social groups. It has recognized the existence of powerful if invisible social forces, and called the origins of those forces real in themselves, not mere aggregates of individuals.

It is hard to appreciate what a breakthrough this may be for the human's concept of itself as a species. So could you please, once more for old time's sake, imagine something for us? Imagine what it must have been like to be a one celled animal when the first multicellular beasties were forming. You were all lining up in circles, passing food to one another, specializing a little bit, becoming interdependent. But you also probably all thought of yourselves as individuals. Rugged ones, undoubtedly, if you had survived up to then. When push came to shove, who did you look out for? Probably you looked out for Number one, Mr. One-Celled Fellow.

Actually, since you the human are a very distant descendant of a surviving multicellular animal, maybe you imagined a different way of being. Maybe you stopped seeing yourself as an individual organism and recognized that there was this group of you, and what you did affected the group, and what the group did affected you. You joined the team and you survived. At first, it must have felt a bit unliberating. Even dangerous, if the group chose to go off and do something that endangered itself or you personally. So some of you learned to let the whole group know when a change in policy was needed (that group of you probably evolved into a primitive nervous system). Then you survived even better.

Today humans may be evolving into a very similar situation on this planet. Our global interdependence and communication among ourselves has grown so tremendously that we almost seem like one whole, in spite of our superficial divisions. Much depends now on our getting through that tricky period when the group moves off, almost randomly, and no one is in charge enough to say, "Hey, that's not a good idea for any of us." We need to develop some of us into social nervous systems, so to speak. And perhaps it is here that social psychologists fit into the picture.

As you have seen, social psychologists are acutely aware of the social reality—that they live within a larger whole—and many are constantly thinking about how they give that whole a better knowledge of itself, how they can guide it better. In this book whole chapters are devoted to these two facets of social psychology, seeing the reality and striving to improve on it. All we are trying to add here is a little more perspective. When social psychologists reflect upon the social world, they may be leading us all toward an expanded awareness that will prove essential to our survival.

Smiling into the Mirror

You have seen in this book that social psychologists, although varied in personality and interests, often show a passion about their work that is perhaps surprising for a scientific discipline. They are not at all shy about taking on the major issues of the ages if that is what they enjoy. Their reality is social and cognitive, both personally and professionally, and they are on an active crusade to make that everyone's reality. Their research is an act of love, their theorizing is as exciting for them as an all night student bull session, and they hope that their work will help build a better world.

In other words, besides all the serious social awareness in social psychology, these people seem to be having a lot of fun. Or at least getting awfully involved. We asked them about it. One of them, Jerry Singer, said it very eloquently: "Social psychology is what I enjoy."

When pushed, he added:

> I can't think of anything else I'd rather do. And people are willing to pay me handsomely for doing it. I can't believe that still. After all these years, when I shave every morning I think, "Today is the day they are going to find me out." Somebody is going to discover, "Hey, we've been paying him to do this."

We asked some social psychologists if they thought it was all right that it was so much fun. But the few times we got a serious answer, it seemed to us that the respondent hadn't understood the question. *Of course* it was all right to have fun, to be involved, to get excited.

This is not the image of science that most scientists grew up with. Scientists are supposed to be serious and objective. Maybe that is why most scientists don't seem to be having much fun.

Except is that true? Maybe some of you have already felt that we've been pulling your leg a little with this argument that social psychology is so much more fun and passionate than the other sciences. Einstein certainly seemed to be enjoying himself. And Madame Curie was totally enthusiastic about chemistry and her wonderful radium. The Leakeys always seemed happiest around their digs. Jacques Cousteau is always beaming. Don't *all* scientists enjoy their work? Don't they all get worked up over their theories? And would Roger Bacon, founder of the science-as-hard-objective-work school, approve?

There are some new answers to all of that, thanks to the reflection of science upon itself through fields called the psychology and sociology of science. In particular, we have enjoyed the ideas of I.J. Mitroff (1974) (a social psychologist of course), who has written a book called *The Subjective Side of Science*, based on his study of NASA lunar scientists. Mitroff concludes that all the best scientists that he studied were very subjectively involved in their work. Further, Mitroff insists that they had to be if they were going to stick it out through all the boring periods and setbacks that arise during a major research project.

Yet these individual, subjective scientists still produce objective scientific knowledge—through the social structure of science. That is, the facts get distilled from all this subjectivity by the larger scientific community. While each scientist may not be able to be entirely objective about his or her own corner of the field, it is still possible for each to be objective about other people's work, when it is close to but outside of their own. Thus with time, the wheat gets separated from the chaff and the truth separated from the polemics, just as we saw in the cognitive dissonance versus self-perception-theory dispute. And the good work gets done because it was fun and exciting, not methodical and dull. Or as Mitroff says,

> For too long one of the myths we have lived with is that science is a passionless enterprise performed by passionless men, and that it *has* to be if it is to be objective. What this myth ignores is that many of

the great scientific achievements of the past have been the result of passionate, if not outright biased, inquiries. . . . science is no less objective because of this passion. Indeed, there are serious reasons for contending that science is more, not less, objective *precisely because of* (and not in spite of) the presence of great passions. (1974, pp. 23–24)

Therefore, if social psychology is more passionate and fun than other sciences, it is certainly not more so than good science in any field, at least according to Mitroff. Perhaps, as with its self-reflection and social awareness, it is merely leading the way a little bit more.

We would like to close with the words of one of social psychology's founders, Muzafer Sherif.

> I disagree completely with those that say that science is aloof, that science should be a cool thing, without emotion. I don't think that there is anybody who has produced anything creative, any Nobel Prize winners in any fields, who haven't felt personally excited about their work, or who haven't been concerned about human beings.
>
> [Social psychology] isn't a job that you go to from nine to five and then quit and forget about it. For me social psychology . . . is value-charged. . . . People in the human sciences . . . should be . . . purely concerned about it . . . not learn psychology like a little trade and do our little technical things and carry on little social activities. The human sciences . . . should develop a keen consciousness of the situation. And then feel to do something about it—not . . . because we have to make a living . . . but [because we are concerned] about the predicament we humans are in today.

Thank you Muzafer. And Kurt, Fritz, Leon, Ellen, Daryl, Elliot, Elaine, Dalmas, Morton, Dorwin, Isodore, Solomon, Herbert, and all the others. (Even your names express your unusual diversity and charm.) Thank you for your daring, your chutzpah. And thank you for having so much heart. May all your ideas be fruitful, your results significant, and your efforts a means of unity.

Appendix

The most appropriate chapters in several current social psychology texts with which to assign chapters from *The Heart of Social Psychology:*

Text	\multicolumn{8}{c}{*The Heart of Social Psychology* Chapter}							
	1	2	3	4	5	6	7	8
Aronson (1984)	1	2, 9	(5)	8	6	7, 9	4	6
Baron & Byrne (1984)	1	7	11	(5, 11)	2, 3	6	4	5, 13
Deaux & Wrightsman (1984)	1	12	14	5	4	6, 2	11, 1	16, 18
Gergen & Gergen (1981)	1	10	12	(11)	2	3	5	(4)
Kahn (1984)	1	9	10	(2)	3, 2	6, 1	5	12
Myers (1983)	1	6, 7	9	(12)	3	13	2	14
Pearlman & Cozby (1983)	1	14	15	(7)	6	8, 2	5	19
Penrod (1983)	1	10	13	7	5	2, 6	8	16
Sherrod (1982)	1	(10)	11	(5, 11)	6	7, 2	5	13
Watson, deBortali-Tregerthan, & Frank (1984)	1	8	9	(9, 12)	2	5, 1	(6, 3)	7

Note: Chapters listed in parentheses only partially overlap with material in *The Heart of Social Psychology* chapter.

References

Allport, F.H. (1924). *Social psychology*. Boston: Houghton Mifflin.

Allport, F.H. (1974). Floyd H. Allport. In G. Lindzey (Ed.), *A history of psychology in autobiography* (Vol. 6, pp. 1–29). Englewood Cliffs, N.J.: Prentice-Hall.

Allport, G.W. (1968). The historical background of modern social psychology. In G. Lindzey & E. Aronson (Eds.,) *The handbook of social psychology* (Vol. 1, 2nd ed., pp. 1–80). Reading, Mass.: Addison-Wesley.

Aron, A. (1970). Relationship variables in human heterosexual attraction. Unpublished doctoral dissertation, University of Toronto.

Aron, A., & Aron, E.N. (1981a). Evidence from Transcendental Meditation research for a social field. In W.J. Reckmeyer (Ed.), *General systems research and design: Precursors and futures* (pp. 316–322). Louisville, Ky.: Society for General Systems Research.

Aron, A., & Aron, E.N. (1981b). Experimental interventions of high coherence groups into disorderly social systems. Paper presented at the annual convention of the American Psychological Association, August, Los Angeles.

Aron, A., & Aron, E.N. (1986). *Love and the expansion of self: Understanding attraction and satisfaction*. New York: Hemisphere.

Aron, E.N., & Aron, A. (1986). *The Maharishi Effect: Revolution through meditation*. Walpole, N.H.: Stillpoint Press.

Aronson, E. (1980). Persuasion via self-justification: Large commitments for small rewards. In L. Festinger (Ed.), *Retrospections on social psychology* (pp. 3–21). New York: Oxford University Press.

Aronson, E. (1984). *The social animal* (4th ed.). San Francisco: W.H. Freeman.

Aronson, E., & Bridgeman, D. (1979). Jigsaw groups and the desegregated classroom: In pursuit of common goals. *Personality and Social Psychology Bulletin, 5,* 438–466.

Aronson, E., & Carlsmith, J.M. (1963). Effect of the severity of threat on the devaluation of forbidden behavior. *Journal of Abnormal and Social Psychology, 66,* 584–588.

Aronson, E., & Mills, J. (1959). The effect of severity of initiation on liking for a group. *Journal of Abnormal and Social Psychology, 59,* 177–181.

Arrowood, A.J. (1978). Social comparison theory: Revived from neglect. *Contemporary Psychology, 23,* 490–491.

Asch, S.E. (1946). Forming impressions of personality. *Journal of Abnormal and Social Psychology, 41,* 258–290.

Asch, S.E. (1958). Effects of group pressure upon the modification and distortion of judgments. In E.E. Maccoby, T.M. Newcomb, & E.L. Hartley (Eds.), *Readings in social psychology* (3rd ed., pp. 174–183). New York: Holt, Rinehart & Winston.

Asch, S.E. (1959). A perspective on social psychology. In S. Kock (Ed.), *Psychology: A study of a science* (Vol. 3, pp. 363–383). New York: McGraw-Hill.

Back, K.W. (1972). *Beyond words: The story of sensitivity training and encounter groups.* New York: Russell Sage Foundation.

Bales, R.F. (1950). *Interaction process analysis: A method for the study of small groups.* Cambridge, Mass.: Addison-Wesley.

Bales, R.F. (1958). Task roles and social roles in problem-solving groups. In E.E. Maccoby, T.M. Newcomb, & E.L. Hartley (Eds.), *Readings in social psychology* (3rd ed., pp. 437–447). New York: Holt, Rinehart & Winston.

Bales, R.F., & Slater, P.E. (1955). Role differentiation in small decision-making groups. In T. Parsons & R.F. Bales (Eds.), *Family, socialization and interaction process* (pp. 259–306). Glencoe, Ill.: The Free Press.

Baron, R., and Byrne, D. (1984). *Social psychology: Understanding human interaction.* Boston: Allyn & Bacon.

Baumrind, D. (1964). Some thoughts on ethics of research: After reading Milgram's "Behavioral study of obedience." *American Psychologist, 19,* 421–423.

Bem, D.J. (1965). An experimental analysis of self-persuasion. *Journal of Experimental Social Psychology, 1,* 199–218.

Bem, D.J. (1967a). Self-perception: An alternative interpretation of cognitive dissonance phenomena. *Psychological Review, 74,* 183–200.

Bem, D.J. (1967b). Reply to Judson Mills. *Psychological Review, 74,* 536–537.

Bem, D.J. (1972). Self-perception theory. In L. Berkowitz (Ed.), *Advances in experimental social psychology* (Vol. 6, pp. 1–62). New York: Academic Press.

Bovard, E.W. (1948). Social norms and the individual. *Journal of Abnormal and Social Psychology, 43,* 62–69.

Brickman, P., Coates, D., & Janoff-Bulman, R. (1978). Lottery winners and accident victims: Is happiness relative? *Journal of Personality and Social Psychology, 36,* 917–927.

Byrne, D. (1971). *The attraction paradigm.* New York: Academic Press.

Cartwright, D. (1978). Theory and practice. *Journal of Social Issues, 34,* 168–180.

Cartwright, D. (1979). Contemporary social psychology in historical perspective. *Social Psychology Quarterly, 42,* 82–93.

Cohen, D. (1977). *Psychologists on psychology.* New York: Taplinger.

Crutchfield, R.S. (1955). Conformity and character. *American Psychologist, 10,* 191–198.

Darley, J.M., & Gross, P.H. (1983). A hypothesis-confirming bias in labeling effects. *Journal of Personality and Social Psychology, 44,* 20–33.

Deaux, K., & Wrightsman, L.S. (1984). *Social psychology in the eighties* (4th ed.). New York: Knopf.

Deutsch, M., & Collins, M.E. (1951). *Interracial housing: A psychological evaluation of a social experiment.* Minneapolis: University of Minnesota Press.

Dillbeck, M.C., Landrith, G., & Orme-Johnson, D.W. (1981). The Transcendental Meditation program and crime rate change in a sample of forty-eight cities. *Journal of Crime and Justice, 4,* 25–46.

Dutton, D. (1971). Reactions of restaurateurs to blacks and whites violating restaurant requirements. *Canadian Journal of Behavioral Science, 3,* 298–302.

Dutton, D.G., & Aron, A.P. (1974). Some evidence for heightened sexual attraction under conditions of high anxiety. *Journal of Personality and Social Psychology, 30,* 510–517.

Ehrlich, D., Guttman, I., Schonbach, P., & Mills, J. (1957). Post-decision exposure to relevant information. *Journal of Abnormal and Social Psychology, 54,* 98–102.

Evans, R.I. (1976). *The making of psychology: Discussions with creative contributors.* New York: Knopf.

Evans, R.I. (1980). *The making of social psychology.* New York: Gardner Press.

Fazio, R.H., Zanna, M.P., & Cooper, J. (1977). Dissonance and self-perception: An integrative view of each theory's proper domain of application. *Journal of Experimental Social Psychology, 13,* 464–479.

Festinger, L. (1954). A theory of social comparison processes. *Human Relations, 7,* 117–140.

Festinger, L. (1957). *A theory of cognitive dissonance.* Stanford, Calif.: Stanford University Press.

Festinger, L., & Carlsmith, J.M. (1959). Cognitive consequences of forced compliance. *Journal of Abnormal and Social Psychology, 58,* 203–210.

Finison, L.J. (1979). An aspect of the early history of the Society for the Psychological Study of Social Issues: Psychologists and Labor. *Journal of the History of the Behavioral Sciences, 15,* 29–37.

Gergen, K.J. (1977). The social construction of self-knowledge. In T. Mischel (Ed.), *The self: Psychological and philosophical issues* (pp. 139–169). Totowa, N.J.: Rowman & Littlefield.

Gergen, K.J., & Gergen, M. (1981). *Social psychology.* New York: Harcourt Brace Jovanovich.

Geiwitz, J., & Moursund, J. (1979). *Approaches to personality.* Monterey, Calif.: Brooks/Cole.

Glass, D.C., & Singer, J.E. (1972). *Urban stress: Experiments on noise and social stressors.* New York: Academic Press.

Gottman, J.M. (1979). *Marital interaction.* New York: Academic Press.

Greenwald, A.G., & Ronis, D.L. (1978). Twenty years of cognitive dissonance: Case study of the evolution of a theory. *Psychological Review, 85,* 53–57.

Haney, C., Banks, C., & Zimbardo, P.G. (1973). Interpersonal dynamics in a simulated prison. *International Journal of Criminology and Penology, 1,* 69–97.

Heider, F. (1958). *The psychology of interpersonal relations.* New York: Wiley.

Heider, F. (1983). *The life of a psychologist.* Lawrence: University Press of Kansas.

Heider, F., & Simmel, M. (1944). An experimental study of apparent behavior. *American Journal of Psychology, 57,* 243–259.

Jacobs, R.C., & Campbell, D.T. (1961). The perpetuation of an arbitrary tradition through several generations of a laboratory microculture. *Journal of Abnormal and Social Psychology, 62,* 649–658.

Janis, I.L. (1972). *Victims of groupthink.* Boston: Houghton Mifflin.

Jones, R.A., Linder, D.E., Kiesler, C.A., Zanna, M., & Brehm, J.W. (1968). Internal states or external stimuli: Observers' attitude judgments and the dissonance theory-self-persuasion controversy. *Journal of Experimental Social Psychology, 4,* 247–269.

Kahn, A. (1984). *Social psychology*. Dubuque, Iowa: William C. Brown.

Kelley, H.H. (1950). The warm–cold variable in first impressions of persons. *Journal of Personality, 18*, 431–439.

Kelley, H.H. (1967). Attribution theory in social psychology. In D. Levine (Ed.), *Nebraska Symposium on Motivation, 1967* (Vol. 15, pp. 192–240). Lincoln: University of Nebraska Press.

Kelley, H.H., & Thibaut, J.W. (1954). Experimental studies in group problem solving and process. In G. Lindzey (Ed.), *Handbook of Social Psychology* (Vol. 2, pp. 735–785). Cambridge, Mass.: Addison-Wesley.

Kelley, H.H., & Thibaut, J.W. (1978). *Interpersonal relations: A theory of interdependence*. New York: Wiley-Interscience.

Kiesler, C.A., & Baral, R. (1970). The search for a romantic partner: The effects of self-esteem and physical attractiveness on romantic behavior. In K. Gergen and D. Marlowe (Eds.), *Psychology and social behavior*. Reading, Mass.: Addison-Wesley.

Krech, D. (1975). David Krech. In G. Lindzey (Ed.), *A history of psychology in autobiography* (Vol. 6, pp. 219–250). Englewood Cliffs, N.J.: Prentice-Hall.

Krech, D., Crutchfield, R.S., & Ballachey, E.L. (1962). *Individual in society: A textbook of social psychology* (3rd ed.). New York: McGraw-Hill.

LaFrance, M., & Mayo, C. (1976). Racial differences in gaze behavior during conversations: Two systematic observational studies. *Journal of Personality and Social Psychology, 33*, 547–552.

Lamberth, J. (1980). *Social Psychology*. New York: Macmillan.

Langer, E.J., & Rodin, J. (1976). The effects of choice and enhanced personal responsibility for the aged: A field experiment in an institutional setting. *Journal of Personality and Social Psychology, 34*, 191–198.

Latane, B., & Darley, J. (1970). *The unresponsive bystander: Why doesn't he help?* New York: Appleton-Century-Crofts.

Lewin, G. (1948). Preface. In D.C. Cartwright (Ed.), *Field theory in social science: Selected theoretical papers by Kurt Lewin* (pp. vii–xiv). New York: Harper & Brothers.

Lewin, K. (1939). Experiments in social space. *Harvard Educational Review, 9*, 21–32.

Lewin, K. (1948). *Resolving social conflicts*. New York: Harper.

Lewin, K. (1951). Field theory and learning. In D.C. Cartwright (Ed.), *Field theory in social science: Selected theoretical papers by Kurt Lewin* (pp. 60–86). New York: Harper & Brothers. (Reprinted from *Yearbook of the National Society for the Study of Education, 1942, Part II*, 215–242).

Lewin, K. (1951). Problems of research in social psychology. In D.C. Cartwright (Ed.), *Field theory in social science: Selected theoretical papers by Kurt Lewin* (pp. 155–169). New York: Harper & Brothers.

Leyens, J-P., Camino, L., Parke, R.D., & Berkowitz, L. (1975). Effects of movie violence on aggression in a field setting as a function of group dominance and cohesion. *Journal of Personality and Social Psychology, 32*, 346–360.

MacKinnon, D.W. (1949). Introductory remarks (Kurt Lewin Memorial Award Meeting). *Journal of Social Issues, 5*, Supplement Series 3, 3–4.

Marrow, A.J. (1969). *The Practical Theorist*. New York: Basic Books.

Mehrabian, A., & Ferris, S.R. (1967). Inference of attitudes from nonverbal communication in two channels. *Journal of Consulting Psychology, 31*, 248–252.

Milgram, S. (1963). Behavioral study of obedience. *Journal of Abnormal and Social Psychology, 67*, 371–378.

Milgram, S. (1964). Issues in the study of obedience: A reply to Baumrind. *American Psychologist, 19*, 848–852.

Miller, G.R., & Burgoon, J.K. (1982). Factors affecting assessments of witness credibility. In N.L. Kerr & R.M. Bray (Eds.), *The psychology of the courtroom* (pp. 169–194). New York: Academic Press.

Mills, J. (1967). Comment on Bem's "Self-perception: An alternative interpretation of cognitive dissonance phenomena." *Psychological Review, 74*, 535.

Mitroff, I.J. (1974). *The subjective side of science*. New York: Elsevier.

Murphy, G. (1965). The future of social psychology in historical perspective. In O. Klineberg & R. Christie (Eds.), *Perspectives in social psychology* (pp. 21–34). New York: Holt, Rinehart & Winston.

Myers, D.G. (1982). Polarizing effects of social interaction. In H. Brandstatter, J.H. Davis, & G. Stocker-Kreichgauer (Eds.), *Group decision making* (pp. 125–161). New York: Academic Press.

Myers, D.G. (1983). *Social psychology*. New York: McGraw-Hill.

Newcomb, T.M. (1947). Autistic hostility and social reality. *Human Relations, I*, 69–86.

Newcomb, T.M. (1958). Attitude development as a function of reference groups. In E.E. Maccoby, T.M. Newcomb, & E.L. Hartley (Eds.), *Readings in social psychology* (3rd ed., pp. 265–275). New York: Holt, Rinehart & Winston.

Newcomb, T.M. (1974). Theodore M. Newcomb. In G. Lindzey (Ed.), *A history of psychology in autobiography* (Vol. 6, pp. 365–391). Englewood Cliffs, N.J.: Prentice-Hall.

Orme-Johnson, D.W., Dillbeck, M.C., Alexander, C.N., Van den Berg, W., & Dillbeck, S.L. (in press). The Vedic psychology of Maharishi Mahesh Yogi. In R.A. Chalmers, G. Clements, H. Shenkluhn, & M. Weinless (Eds.), Scientific research on the Transcendental Meditation and TM–Sidhi programme: Collected papers (Vol. 4). Rheinweiller, Federal Republic of Germany: MERU Press.

Pearlman, D., & Cozby, P.C. (1983). *Social psychology*. New York: Holt, Rinehart & Winston.

Penrod, S. (1983). *Social psychology*, Englewood Cliffs, N.J.: Prentice-Hall.

Rodin, J., & Langer, E.J. (1977). Long-term effects of control-relevant intervention with the institutionalized aged. *Journal of Personality and Social Psychology, 35*, 897–902.

Rogers, C.R. (1968). Interpersonal relationships, USA. *Journal of Applied Behavioral Science, 4*, 265–280.

Rohrer, J.H., Baron, S.H., Hoffman, E.L., & Swander, D.V. (1954). The stability of autokinetic judgments. *Journal of Abnormal and Social Psychology, 9*, 595–597.

Rosenthal, R., & Fode, K.L. (1963). The effect of experimenter bias on the performance of the albino rat. *Behavioral Science, 8*, 183–189.

Rosenthal, R., & Jacobson, L.F. (1968). Teacher expectations for the disadvantaged. *Scientific American, 218*, 19–23.

Ross, L.D., Amabile, T.M., & Steinmetz, J.L. (1977). Social roles, social control, and biases in social-perception processes. *Journal of Personality and Social Psychology*, 35, 485–494.

Rubin, Z. (1970). Measurement of romantic love. *The Journal of Personality and Social Psychology*, 10, 265–273.

Schachter, S. (1959). *The psychology of affiliation*. Stanford, Calif.: Stanford University Press.

Schachter, S., & Singer, J. (1962). Cognitive, social, and physiological determinants of emotional state. *Psychological Review*, 69, 379–399.

Schultz, D. (1975). *A history of modern psychology* (2nd ed.). New York: Academic Press.

Sears, D.O., & Abeles, R.P. (1969). Attitudes and opinions. In P.H. Mussen and M.R. Rosenzweig (Eds.), *Annual Review of Psychology* (Vol. 20, pp. 253–288). Palo Alto, Calif.: Annual Reviews.

Sherif, M. (1935). A study of some social factors in perception. *Archives of Psychology*, 27, No. 187, 1–60.

Sherif, M. (1966). *In common predicament: Social psychology of intergroup conflict and cooperation*. Boston: Houghton Mifflin.

Sherif, M., Harvey, O.J., White, B.J., Hood, W.E., & Sherif, C.W. (1961). *Intergroup conflict and cooperation: The Robber's Cave experiment*. Norman: University of Oklahoma Book Exchange.

Sherif, M., & Sherif, C.W. (1969). *Social psychology*. New York: Harper & Row.

Sherif, M., & Sherif, C.W. (1973). *Groups in harmony and tension: An integration of studies on intergroup relations*. New York: Octagon.

Sherrod, D. (1982). *Social psychology*. New York: Random House.

Snyder, M., Tanke, E.D., & Berscheid, E. (1977). Social perception and interpersonal behavior: The self-fulfilling nature of social stereotypes. *Journal of Personality and Social Psychology*, 35, 656–666.

Slater, P.E. (1955). Role differentiation in small groups. In A.P. Hare, E.F. Borgatta, & R.F. Bales (Eds.), *Small groups: Studies in social interaction* (pp. 498–515). New York: Knopf.

Strickland, L.H., Aboud, F.E., & Gergen, K.J. (1976). The "power structure" in social psychology. In *Social psychology in transition* (pp. 307–316). New York: Plenum.

Tesser, A. (1978). Self-generated attitude change. In L. Berkowitz (Ed.), *Advances in experimental social psychology* (Vol. 11, pp. 289–338). New York: Academic Press.

Thibaut, J.W., & Kelley, H.H. (1959). *The social psychology of groups*. New York: Wiley.

Tolman, E.C. (1948). Kurt Lewin—1890–1947. *Journal of Social Issues*, 4, 22–26.

Triplett, N. (1898). The dynamogenic factors in pacemaking and competition. *American Journal of Psychology*, 9, 507–533.

Tuddenham, R.D., & Macbride, P. (1959). The yielding experiment from the subject's point of view. *Journal of Personality*, 27, 259–271.

Valins, S. (1966). Cognitive effects of false heart-rate feedback. *Journal of Personality and Social Psychology*, 4, 400–408.

Walster, E., Aronson, V., Abrahams, D., & Rottman, L. (1966). Importance of physical attractiveness in dating behavior. *Journal of Personality and Social Psychology, 4,* 508–516.

Watson, J.B. (1913). Psychology as the behaviorist views it. *Psychological Review, 20,* 158–177.

Watson, D.L., deBortali-Tregerthan, G., & Frank, J. (1984). *Social psychology: Science and application.* Glenview, Ill.: Scott, Foresman.

Weick, K.E., & Gilfillan, D.P. (1971). Fate of arbitrary traditions in a laboratory microculture. *Journal of Personality and Social Psychology, 17,* 179–191.

Zajonc, R.B. (1980). Cognition and social cognition: A historical perspective. In L. Festinger (Ed.), *Retrospections on social psychology* (pp. 180–204). New York: Oxford University Press.

Zimbardo, P.G. (1969). The human choice: Individuation, reason, and order versus deindividuation, impulse, and chaos. In W.J. Arnold and D. Levine (Eds.), *Nebraska Symposium on Motivation, 1969* (Vol. 17, pp. 237–308). Lincoln: University of Nebraska Press.

Zimbardo, P.G. (1985). *Psychology and life* (11th ed.). Glenview, Ill.: Scott, Foresman.

Zuckerman, M., DePaulo, B.M., & Rosenthal, R. (1981). Verbal and nonverbal communication of deception. *Journal of Personality and Social Psychology, 43,* 347–357.

Index

About the Authors

ARTHUR Aron (B.A., psychology and philosophy, University of California, 1967; M.A., psychology, University of California, 1968; Ph.D., University of Toronto, 1970) previously held positions at the University of British Columbia, University of Paris (Laboratoire de Psychologie Sociale), Maharishi International University, and Institute for Advanced Research. Currently he is dividing his time between writing, research, and teaching (at the University of Santa Clara and the University of California at Santa Cruz).

Elaine N. Aron (B.A., Phi Beta Kappa, psychology, University of California, 1968; M.A., psychology, York University, 1970) has done counseling, trained counselors, and held academic positions at Maharishi International University and the Institute for Advanced Research. Currently she is mostly writing, plus teaching part-time at Chapman College and the University of Santa Clara.

Together the Arons have published or presented at scientific meetings more than seventy papers on their research, which focuses on personal relationships, the social effects of meditation, creativity, emotions, and social change. They live together in Capitola, California, with their son, Elijah.